LAUKIKANYĀYAKOŚA

लौकिकन्यायकोश

LAUKIKANYĀYAKOŚA

लौकिकन्यायकोश

Dr. P. G. Lalye

BKP

BHARATIYA KALA PRAKASHAN

DELHI (INDIA)

First Edition : 2006

Published by **C.P. Gautam**
BHARATIYA KALA PRAKASHAN
3421-A, IInd Floor Narang Colony, Tri Nagar,
Delhi-110035. Phone : 27393083, 32967505 (O), 32492129 (R)

ISBN : 81-8090-142-4

Laser Type Setting by
A-ONE GRAPHICS
JD-18C, IInd Floor, Pitampura, Delhi-110088.

Printed By :
BDH Printer at Salasar Imaging Systems.

Laukikanyāyakośa

(An Anthology of Popular Maxims)

The word Nyāya has so many connotative facets in Sanskrit and in other Indian languages that one has to ascertian the exact connotation of Nyāya in the concerned work. Though Nyāya often means justice, it expresses many more meanings. Infact, Apte's Dictionary has assigned the following twelve sets of meaning to this word.

(i) Method, manner

(ii) Fitness, propriety

(iii) Low, justice, Virtue, equity, righteousness.

(iv) A law suit,

(v) Judicial sentence,

(vi) Policy, good government

(vii) A popular maxim

(viii) An opposite illustration,

(ix) Vedic account.

(x) A universal rule.

(xi) System of Hindu philosophy founded by the sage Gautama.

(xii) Syllogism—An epithet of Viṣṇu

The word is well-known in the sense of "the science of Logic". It is also well-known as a group of words conveying some incidents or events, based on worldly dealings or experiences. Such group of words is also called a maxim or an adage. As it is strongly based on the behaviour of worldly beings, the word (maxim), the ultimate or the final word of which is Nyāya. It also conveys some special type of behaviour not only of the human being but also of the birds and animals. The maxim, thus formed, does not always directly indicate the pattern of behaviour, unless the pattern involved is expatiated. Thus many Nyāyas are properly understood by the references to the context of the anecdotes or events.

The Śāstras Sūtras are very brief and some what incomprehensible at the beginning. So also the maxims are brief, mostly embodied in one compound with vague or concealed incidents. The maxim can be reframed into a sentence with a slight change. Nyāya is connected with the group of words where in the Nyāya converts some incident into an adage. It is, however, endowed with some significance.

A Nyāya can be contrasted with an idiom. The Advance Oxford dictionary defines an idiom as a phrase or a sentence whose meaning is not clear from the meaning of its individual words and which must be learnt as a whole unit. The maxim or a Nyāya is the crystalization of some event or a legend. Buhler calls the Nyāya as the inferences from familiar utterances. The Oxford diction defines maxim as a saying that expresses a general truth or a rule of conduct. There are such maxims in English as well as in other languages but they are crystalized in Nyāya type phrases of Sanskrit. The Nyāyas are condensed legends, throwing light on the human behaviour (and that of other beings also). The Nyāyas permeates wide spheres of human beings, animals, trees and even inanimate objects. Some scholars have tried to collect as many maxims as possible and have given explanations, based on their usages in several Sanskrit works.

Colonel G.A. Jacob has collected Nyāyas which are

combined in one volume (the book is published by Niranjanā publishers and Book sellers, New Delhi, 1983). These Nyāyas are chosen from various fields including the S'āstric works. They encompass different types of beliefs, principles or articles of faith, minor experiences, canons, deeds, crescendos, catechisms etc. They underline some popular legends prevalent in folklores which are surrounded with classical aura. As they are prudent in nature, they enrich the literature and give it a didactic tinge.

The Nyāya gives some suggested sense. Thus it might have been clear that a variety of experiences constitute the main story of the Nyāya or the maxim. In course of time, the experiences were crystalized in ever growing manner in the conversations, in different regions, different action-reaction plans. The efflorescence of human mind with all its glories and dark sides have shaped various maxims. Any maxim presupposes three stages—(i) the experience, (ii) couching the experience briefly in words and then (iii) casting searching light on human behaviour. The maxims, however, become impersonal. As such, they attain an abiding place in the human communications and in the folk literature too and then to the classical literature.

The next problem is the classification of the maxims under probable heads. Some broad method of classification is suggested by the author of the oldest anthology of the Nyāyas-Bhuvaneśalaukikanyāya sāhasrī.

ये चात्र लौकिकन्यायाः प्रोक्तास्तेषामुदाहृतिः।
वेदान्तशास्त्रगा काचित् कचिच्च शब्दशास्त्रगां।।६।।
काचिभ्यायानुगा काचिन्मीमांसा शास्त्र गा तथा।
लौकिकोक्तिर्यथा तद्वत् प्रायः प्रोक्ताऽपरापिवा।।७।।
अर्थमात्रं क्वचित्तेषामर्थे स्पष्टे स्फुटं स्मृतम्।
प्रायः सङ्क्षेपतः प्रोक्तं विस्तरादपि च क्वचित्।।८।।

Thakura Datta Sharma, the editor of the works, has given an alphabetical list of all the Nyāyas at the beginning. He has tried to find out a common link in the body of the works, wherever possible, to cluster the Nyāyas together. The book, printed in 1908, is the oldest printed colleclion of the Nyāyas. The writer has exhaustively quoted from the Sanskrit literature including the Sūtras of Pāṇinī. He has cited lines containing some popular beliefs at some places e.g. कार्यात् कारणजन्मेतिन्यायः– in which the lines—

लता हि शैले-सरसि भवम् सरोजम्-पुष्पाणां प्रभवो वै।

are quoted, though the original works in which their occurances are not traceable. Thus with a fine exegetical skill, Thakura Datta Sharma has enriched the selection.

Explanations of certain Nyāyas occurs in certain commentorial works but they are only incidental and cannot be designated as Nyāyakośas.

Nyāyakośa work which is now available is- लौकिकन्यायाञ्जलि A handful of popular maxims are published in three parts during the period 1900-1904. Jacob has explained in these tracts the maxims, quoting lines from the classical as well as from the Śāstric works. He has prepared an enlarged version during 1907-1911, in which the total number of Nyāyas was 484. I have considered this collection of the maxims as the most dependable one.

The next available work on the Nyāyas is the "Nyāyokti-kośa"—published by Chavinath Mishra in 1978. They have been discussed in Sanskrit only.

Prof. Dr. R. Srihari, Retired Vice-Chancellor, Dravidian University, Kuppam—a well-known Telugu. Sanskrit scholar, has written a Nyāyakośa in Telugu. It was published by Surabharati Samiti, Hyderabad in 1993. This work has been of immense inspiration and help to me in the preparation of this work.

The work of Colonel Jacob was an ideal before me. I have adopted his discussion (with slight changes) in interpreting the Nyāyas. He has taken illustrations from various works like 'Vācaspatya', the works of Satyavrata Sāmāśrami and Raghunātha Varmā. He has appended a list of Nyāyas, arranged in alphabetical order in Devanagari script. One more book has been recently published which has discussed Nyāyas from the Mahābhāṣya of Patanjali.

The Nyāyas may be classified mainly under the following topics:—

1. Nyāyas related to mountains etc.
2. Nyāyas related to ladies.
3. Nyāyas related to rural situations.
4. Nyāyas like Arundhatidarśan nyāya,
5. Nyāyas related to social conditions.
6. Nyāyas like Brāhmaṇa Vasiṣṭha nyāya.
7. Nyāyas like Danḍāpūpa nyāya.
8. Nyāyas related to food articles etc.
9. Nyāyas related to animals and birds
10. Nyāyas like Gobalivardanyāya, Hansaksirodaknyāya.
11. Nyāyas like Khalekapota nyāya.
12. Nyāyas concerning deities.
13. Nyāyas concerning Śāstra conventions.
14. Nyāyas like Nāgṛhitaviśeṣaṇa nyāya, Sandanśa nyāya.
15. Nyāyas related to Agriculture etc.

The early Śāstra writers have added the word Nyāya to certain epigrammatic Śāstra rules, like फल्वत् सन्निघानफल तदङ्गम्।

Cf. (Śabara's commentary on Jaimini vii.2.13). Many such examples have been given by Dr. P.V. Kane in his history of Dharmaśāstra, Vol. V, part II, pp. 1339-1359. This is my humble attempt of collecting the Nyāyas although there are limitations also.

This work is an attempt of placing together the work done by earlier scholars briefly. As far as possible, I have assigned at least one illustration for one Nyāya. I have taken some illustrations mainly from the book "Bhuvaneśanyāya sāhasrī". If a sustained effort is made, many more Nyāyas and illustrations can be collected. Unfortunately, I have to restrict myself to a few ones only. I implore the scholars to look at this work as an effort of summarizing the earlier works. This work has incorporated the treatment of Nyāyas, carried out by the three works—

(i) Bhuvaneśalaukika nyāya sāhasrī,

(ii) Jacob's collection of popular maxims and

(iii) Prof. R. Srihari's Laukikanyāyakośa. I have only taken bath in this Triveṇī sangama. I have freely utilized the sacred water of the confluence.

Needless to say that there is little originality in it. I will deem myself fortunate, if more exhaustive collections of Nyāyas are brought out by the scholars.

Acknowledgement

I gratefully acknowledge the help rendered by the following scholars in preparing this work. I am highly obliged to all of them. I thank Prof. R. Srihari, retired Vice-Chancellor of Dravidian University, Kuppam (A.P) for permitting me to use his book. I am also thankful to Prof. K.S. Arjunwadkar, a versatile scholar of Maharashtra for allowing me to use his books especially the Bhuvaneśa-laukikasāhasrī. Dr. Prasad Joshi prepared a consolidated copy of all the Nyāyas and my revered friend Prof. Y.S. Kulkarni has gone through the work and has given his valuable suggestions wherever needed. I thank both these scholars for their help. The tedious work of proof-correction was undertaken by Prof. Dr. Kanchan Mande, Head dept. of Sanskrit, S.P. College, Pune. Inspite of her tight schedule she willingly agreed to give a helping hand in preparing a list of all the Nyāyas in Devanāgari alphabetical order and thus upholding the motto निर्वाहः प्रतिपन्नवस्तुषु of her institution. I thank her sincerly.

I also thank sincerly Shri Gautambhai—Bharatiya Kala Prakashan, Delhi for undertaking the task of printing and publishing this book. I express my indebtedness to all of them.

लौकिक न्याय कोश
(Laukikanyāyakośa)

1. अक्षिपात्रन्यायः

Just as a little, minute dust particle when fallen into the eye, causes irritation, similarly even a small and trivial trouble causes much suffering to a man of delicate and sentimental nature.

2. अक्ष्याप्तभेषजन्यायः

If the medicine meant for applying to the eyes is applied to the testicles, it will not give any effect. It will become useless. The maxim suggests this act of purposeless deed, having no effect. It also means that though the pupil of the eye is very small, it can see the most subtle things.

3. अगतिकगतिन्यायः

A person who is in distress, tries to extricate himself from that difficult situation by taking help of anything weak or otherwise which is at hand. Here time is given more importance than means.

4. अग्निकुण्डन्यायः

A Brahmin wanted to perform a sacrifice. In order to keep the material at hand, he kept all the material required for the sacrifice, including the fire, in a jar, with the idea of collecting all the things at one place.

But everything was burnt down when he came to that place, the next morning. The nature of the dull-witted fellows who have no knowledge about the worldly affairs is described here.

5. **अग्निशलभन्यायः**

Attracted by the light, a glow-worm jumps on the flame and is completely burnt down. The maxim suggests that doing something rashly and submitting oneself to ephemeral lure, leads one to ruin.

6. **अग्निशिखान्यायः**

As the flame of the fire always goes up, it is also natural for the soul to go upwards. This is suggested in "Sarvadarśana Samgraha"—a book by the Jain philosophers. This work gives four illustrations of the natural movements of the following things:—

(i) Rotation of a potter's wheel.

(ii) Floating on water of a gourd whose mud cover is removed.

(iii) The fallen seed of a castor tree goes up and sticks to the tree.

(iv) The upward surge of a flame.

7. **अग्न्यानयनन्यायः**

When somebody is asked to bring fire, he fetches it in some pot or vessel, even though he is not specifically told to bring it in a vessel. The substratum and the substrated are inseparable.

8. **अङ्कोलबीजन्यायः**

The seeds of the Ankola tree fall down but peculiarly enough, they go back and cling to the tree after the rain-showers in Mṛgaśiras. This suggests that any object or any individual can restore its or his original position in favourable environment, despite the fact that they had fallen down earlier.

9. अङ्गारन्यायः

If the burning charcoal is placed in the hand, the hand gets burnt. If it is touched when it is cooled down, the hand becomes black and dirty. Coal, in any state, is harmful. Similary, the company of the wicked persons is always harmful.

10. अङ्गुलिदीपिकाध्वान्तध्वंसन्यायः

A small little lamp of the size of a finger can remove the darkness. Some people use a big torch to remove the darkess. But how far and to what extent can it obliterate the darkness? It is impossible to remove the darkness completely. This maxim suggests that even a small device may bring about big effect.

11. अचलचलन्यायः

Sometimes a static thing seems to be moving or stationary. When this kind of delusion is caused, this maxim is employed. This kind of delusion is caused when one moves in a running vehicle. The objects which are passed en route, seem to be moving. Many a time, one gets a delusion that the moving boat is still. Similarly a fast moving top seems to be static and the blades of the fast moving fan are invisible. Thus this maxim states that a delusion is caused regarding moving and non-moving objects too.

12. अज्झलन्यायः

Example–एकाकिनोऽपि राजन्ते सारसत्त्वाः स्वरा इव। व्यञ्ज-नानीव निःसत्त्वाः परेषामनुगामिनः॥ –सा० 934

In Sanskrit also, there are two types of letters, vowels

and consonants. Consonants cannot be articulated without the help of vowels. The consonants (Hals) are powerless without vowels (Acs). This maxim is used when dependence of one on some other is to be indicated.

13. अजगरन्यायः

Due to the long and heavy body, it is difficult for a boa to move about. So any creature which comes near it by chance, it swallows it. Similarly, a crane waits silently for a chance to catch a fish which comes within the range of catching.

14. अजहत्स्वार्थवृत्तिन्यायः

'Vṛtti' is the function of a word by which the meaning of a word is conveyed by some another word. When some primary meanings give up their meaning-this function of conveying secondary meaning is called 'Jahatsvãrtha'. Patañjali has dealt with this topic in his commentary on Paṇinian sūtra. "Samarthaḥ Padavidhi" —this function is one of the functions of Lakṣaṇā by which secondary meaning is conveyed, without the original sense being given up.

15. अजाकृपाणीयन्यायः

It a she-goat and a knife happen to come together, it is the she-goat which suffers and not the knife-When something happens accidentally, this maxim is used.This accidental and unknowing happenings are also indicated in "Kākatāliya" and "Khalvāṭa bilvīya" nyāyas.

16. अजागलस्तनन्यायः

धर्मार्थकाममोक्षाणां यस्यैकोऽतिप न विद्यते।
अजागलस्तनस्येव तस्य जन्म निरर्थकम्।।

—ब्रह्माण्डपुरुष, अ० 150; सा० 582

A piece of flesh hangs under the neck of a goat. It has

no role to perform in the bodily functions of a goat. This maxim is used to point out such useless or purposeless things.

17. **अजाण्डपरीक्षान्यायः**

How many testicles does a goat have? How are they or how do they look ? All these are useless questions. This maxim is used for describing similar questions.

18. **अजातपुत्रनामोत्कीर्तनन्यायः**

To praise the virtues of an unborn son and sometimes, even to christen him before his birth, shows the unnecessary haste which is indicated in this maxim.

19. **अजायुद्धन्यायः** Cf.—**प्रभातमेघन्यायः**

The fight between the goats starts with forceful attacks but their force is reduced gradually and everything ends in peace. Similar situation which appears violent but ends in peace, is envisaged by this maxim.

20. **अण्डकुक्कुटीन्यायः**

There is an unanswerable question, who is the earlier one— a hen or an egg? Similarly the question is—which is earlier,. a seed or a sprout ? There seems to be cause-effect relation, ultimately.

21. **अण्डविस्त्रम्भन्यायः**

This maxim is employed to describe a situation when somebody does an adventurous act, believing someone unreasonably or when someone commits a rash action thoughtlessly.

22. **अतिदेशन्यायः**

1. **एकत्र श्रुतस्यान्यत्र सम्बन्धः। अन्यधर्मस्यान्यत्रारोपणम्।**

—सर्वतन्त्रसिद्धान्तपदार्थ लक्षणसङ्ग्रह, पृ० 9

2. **अन्यसम्बन्धिनां धर्माणामन्यत्रावस्थापनमतिदेशः।**

—तन्त्रयुक्तिविचार, पृ० 2

3. **एकत्र श्रुतस्थान्यत्र सम्बन्धः। अन्यधर्मस्यान्यत्रारोपणम्।।**

(i) अतिक्रमणेनातिदेशः —विष्णुधर्मोत्तरपुराणः, पृ० 13

(ii) अतिदेशस्तु यत् किञ्चिदर्थजातमुदीर्य च।
एवमन्यदपि ज्ञेयमिति स्थापनमुक्तिभिः।।
इदत्यतिदेशः। —तन्त्रयुक्ति, पृ० 14

(iii) अतिदेशस्तु पूर्वोक्तन्यायस्थानुषङ्गितः।
—तन्त्रयुक्तिविचार, पृ० 8

This maxim presupposes the extended application of some statement which is stated before. Sometimes the same statement is extended.

Prof. V.K. Lele has the following explanation to offer—(Extention of application to analogous topics). connecting the properties of one with those of the other or superimposing of one upon those of the other is 'atideśa'.

Prof. Lele has cited many definitions of "atideśa". Some of them are given below—.

(i) अतिदेशस्तु पूर्वोक्तन्यायस्यसान्यानुषाङ्गिता।
—नीलमेघऽतन्त्रयुक्ति विचार, पृ० 87

(ii) अतिदेशो नाम यत्किञ्चिदेव प्रकाश्यार्थमनुक्तार्थासधनायैव एकमन्यदपि प्रत्येतव्यमिति परिभास्यते। चरक संहिता I, p. 103 (Prof. W.K. lele, *The Doctrine of the Tantrayukti*, p. 36-37).

23. अतिपरिचयन्यायः

अतिपरिचयादवज्ञा सन्ततगमनादरो भवति।
मलये भिल्लपुरन्ध्री चन्दनतरुकाष्ठमिन्धनं कुरुते।।
—सुभाषित, शार्ङ्गधरणपद्धति नीति 83

'Familiarity breeds contempt'—is the implication of this

maxim. The Bhillas use scented, expensive sandal wood as firewood because they get it easily and in plenty on the Malaya mountain. They do not think about the value of the sandal and burn it like ordinary firewood—This is an example of too much of familiarity leading to contempt.

24. **अतीतमहिषीस्नेहन्यायः**

A person owned a buffalo. He loved that buffalo very much. As days passed, he decided to retire from Gṛhasthāśrama and enter Vānaprasthāśrama. (life of detachment). One has to leave everything in this stage of life. But this person could not give up his love, affection or attachment for the buffalo. This indicates that old ties are difficult to be asundered.

25. **अदग्धदहनन्यायः**

Fire can burn things which are not already burnt. It cannot burn the things already burnt. Patañjali has employed this maxim while commenting on a sūtra of Pāṇini.

26. **अधिकरणसिद्धान्तन्यायः**

Example—**यमर्थमधिकृत्योच्यते तदधिकरणम्।**

—कौटिल्य अर्थशास्त्र, पृ० 4

Adhikaraṇa (topic) is a systematic arrangement of discussion or treatment about a topic. It contains five stages:- subject, doubt, prima facie views, the final view of the arguer and the final conclusion. The maxim is applied to a situation wherein one theory is advanced to substantiate the previous one.

27. **अधिकारन्यायः**

Example—किञ्चित्तु पुरुषविशेषणत्वेन श्रुतमप्यधिकारिविशेषणं भवति।

यथाध्ययनसिद्धा विद्या, अग्निसाध्येषुच, कर्मसु आधान सिद्धाग्निमत्व सामर्थ्यं च। —मीमासान्यायप्रकाश

This maxim is applied where the rules or qualifications, concerning the eligibility of a performer of the sacrifice are mentioned.

28. **अध्यारोपापवादन्यायः**

वस्तुन्यवस्त्वारोपोऽध्यारोपः।
यथा असर्पभूतायां रज्जौ सर्पारोपः।
अपवादो नाम रज्जुविवर्तस्थ सर्पस्य रज्जुमात्रत्ववद् वस्तुविवर्तस्याऽवस्तुनोऽज्ञानादेः प्रपञ्चस्य वस्तुमात्रत्वमिति। ....ताभ्यामध्यारोपावादाभ्यां निष्प्रपञ्चं सच्चिदानन्दनन्ताद्वय ब्रह्म, प्रपञ्च्यते, विस्तार्यते इति भावः।

This maxim envisages two aspects of perception. 'Apavāda' is that act in which absolutely a different concept is imposed on an object. When a wrong imputation is refuted, it is called Apavāda. According to Vedānta, these two operations help one, to arrive at the right knowledge of the Supreme.

29. **अनवस्थान्यायः** Cf. **देहलीदीपन्यायः**

तस्मादर्थान्तर समवायमभ्युपगच्छतः प्रसज्येतैवानवस्था।

—ब्रह्मसूत्र, शाङ्करभाष्य 2-2-13.

When the matter to be proved and the manner in which it is proved, become endless (i-e-reaches a stage of impasse), this maxim becomes applicable to that situation. It is also called reductio ad absurdum.

30. **अनारभ्याधीतविधिन्यायः**

When a particular injunction is not related to a particular topic, the injunction is concerned with the natural import only. Thus when that is not applicable to a particular matter and when there is no earlier reference to it, this maxim comes into picture.

31. **अनेकान्तवादन्यायः**

This maxim suggests uncertainty (indefiniteness). The word Anekānta is used in Jaina philosophy which describes seven possibilities of uncertainty. Some uncertainties can be spoken about Fate.

32. **अनेकाश्रयन्यायः**

This maxim conveys a message that it is better to take support of one strong man than resorting to many weak fellows.

33. **अतरङ्गबहिरङ्गन्यायः**

Examle—यं धर्मा अपूर्वाथस्ति साक्षादपूर्वेण सम्बध्यमानोस्तदङ्गेषु प्रवर्तमाना अन्तरङ्गे तावदापतन्ति। ततो प्यवहिते बाहिरङ्गे। यत्रव पूर्वमापतति तत्रैव तिष्ठति, तरतिक्रमे कारण भावात्।

—शाबरभाष्य जै०सू०, XII.2.11,पाणिनि I.1.4.1.15.

The closer i.e., proximity aspect of anything is stronger than the remote (or external) aspect of it. This rule is often referred to in grammar and Mīmāmsā.

34. **अन्तर्दीपिकान्यायः** example—सत्येन लभ्यस्तपसा ह्येष आत्मा सम्यग्तानेन ब्रह्मचर्येण नित्यम्। मुण्डकोपनिषद्

A lamp, though kept in a jar, illumines at least some portion of the jar and the light spreads out in all the four directions. This maxim is used to describe a person who performs various tasks, remaining at one place.

35. **अन्धकरदीपिकान्यायः**

A mirrror or a lamp is of no use to a blind man. If a person is incapable of using or appreciating the qualities of a particular thing, it is useless for him. This is the purport of this maxim.

36. अन्धकवर्तकीयन्यायः

संसारसागरमिमं भ्रमता नितान्तं
जीवेन मानवभवः समवापि दैवात्।
तत्रापि यद् भुवनमान्यकुले प्रसूतिः
सत्सङ्गतिश्च तदिहान्धकवर्तकीयम्॥ —सा० 655

A blind man was clapping his hand aimlessly, Incidentally a bird called Vartika (a kind of quail) got caught up in his hands. Fortunately,without any effort or without any idea he got the bird. This is a rare happening. Similarly in our life also, many things happen due to our good luck or by coincidence.

37. अन्धकूपन्यायः

Once a blind man was asked to go straight. But he connived at this advice and ultimately fell in a ditch. This maxim suggests that he who does not abide by wholesome advice, is sure to face peril.

—सा० 493

38. अन्धगजन्यायः

Some blindmen were sitting together. A man with his elephant came there.He asked the blind persons to describe the animal. Some blindmen touched his pillar-like feet, some his winnowing basket-like ears, some his long tusk and some his little tail at the back, and began to describe the elephant accordingly. As all of them could not see the animal, they could not give a complete, integrated picture of the elephant. The maxim throws light on the people who have partial knowledge of certian thing and think that the entire thing exists like that.

—सा० 76

39. अन्धगोलाङ्गूलन्यायः

यदि यज्ञस्य सतोः मुमुक्षोरचेतमात्मानत्मेत्युपदिशेत् प्रमाणभूतं शास्त्रं स श्रद्धधानतया अन्धगोलाङ्गूलन्यायेन तदाऽत्मदृष्टि न परित्यजेत्, तद् व्यतिरिक्तं चात्मानं न प्रतिपद्येते। —ब्रह्मसूत्र, शाङ्करभाष्य 1.7, सा० 40

A blindman who was moving falteringly on a street, was advised by an ordinary man to catch hold of the tail of a cow to reach home. Even though the blind man moved about catching the cow's tail in the whole town, he could not reach home. An innocent person is often deceived by a shrewd man. This is the indication of this maxim.

40. अन्धचटकन्यायः

Once a sparrow was caught in the hands of a blindman. The blind man began to blare out, "I have caught a sparrow. Look a sparrow has been caught by me". This maxim describes those who want to take the credit of the deeds which are not acually performed by them.

41. अन्धदर्पणन्यायः

A blindman has no use of a mirror. He cannot see his face in it and use it. This maxim suggests that it is useless to offer something to a person for whom it is of no use.

42. अन्धपङ्गुन्यायः

See (i) तन्त्रवार्तिक, पृ० 11, 72, 75, 232, 799, 897.

(ii) शांकरभाष्य, पृ० 250, 254.

(iii) न्यायमञ्जरी, पृ० 234, 249, 251, 425, 492; सा० 179

Once a blind man and a lame man came together accidentally. Both of them could not move about independently, as the blind was unable to see and the lame could not walk. They thought of a trick. The blind man took the lame man on his shoulder who could guide him, and show him the proper path. With the co.operation of both of them, they were able to reach their destined place. This maxim is made use of in many philosophical works.

43. अन्धपरम्परान्यायः

अनादित्वेऽपि अन्धपरम्परान्यायेनाप्रतिष्ठैवानवस्थाव्यवहार-लोपिनी स्यान्नाभिप्रायसिद्धिः। —सा० 24

(i) A blind man does work which is done likewise by another blindman and it is followed by another blindman and so on .

(ii) Sometimes this maxim describes a situation when nothing is steady and the instability persists. This is called contingency of endlessness.

44. अन्धाक्षिमीलन्यायः

In the case of certain persons, the physical movements do not bring about any change in their personality. Closing of the eyes is not of any significance to a blind man.

45. अन्धाञ्जनयायः

This maxim suggests that ineffective device should not be used. It is futile to apply collyrium to the eyes of a blind man.

46. अन्धानन्दन्यायः

A blind man may be joyful in two situations:–

(i) When his blindness disappears or (ii) When he becomes a Yogin and gets the supreme bliss of realizing the Truth.

47. अन्धानन्धन्यायः

तं वा एतं सेतुं तीर्त्वाऽन्धः सन्ननन्धो भवति।

—छान्दोग्य उप० 8.4.1

A blindman may have his sight restored. This maxim is used in the case of a person who gets enlightenment when his ignorance disappears.

48. अन्धाश्वमौलिन्यायः

This maxim tells that physical deformity of a man does not prove to be an impediment in his eating habits. Even a blind horse eats well.

49. अन्यकारुकान्यायः

A person, born in bad atmosphere, cherishes bad sentiments only, as an insect which takes its birth in dirt, eats rubbish only.

50. अपराह्णछायान्यायः

आरम्भगुर्वी क्षयिणी क्रमेण
लध्वी पुरा वृद्धिमती च पश्चात्।
दिनस्य पूर्वार्धपरार्धभिन्ना
छायेव मैत्री खलसज्जनानाम्।।

—भर्तृहरि, नीतिशतक, 49; सा० 332

This maxim is based on the shadow in the afternoon which grows in length till the evening and then becomes weak slowly thereafter. Similarly the company of the wicked is very intimate in the beginning but gets reduced in the course of time.

51. अपसारिताग्निभूतलन्यायः Cf. चम्पकपटन्यायः

Though fire is shifted from one place to another, the original place remains warm for sometime. Similary, the maxim says that a man may change his place but retains his good or bad quality marks or impressions in the original place.

52. अपृच्छोत्तरन्यायः

The maxim observes that answering an unasked question is the sign of lack of discretion.

53. अप्रसक्तनिषेधन्यायः

The maxim observes that there is some chance of prohibition when one sentence is related to the other. There is no possibility of any prohibition in connection with the unconnected sentences.

54. अब्धिफेनादिन्यायः

The waves and the foam which arise in the ocean, appear to be different from the sea. The projective illusion in the ocean makes foam and waves appear differently. The same māyā or delusion displays many worldly things in the Brahman. The extension in the form and name is illusory. This is the main thrust of the present maxim. –सा० 636

55. अब्भक्षन्यायः "Drinking water only."

Not drinking water may happen in two ways—

i) Not drinking water after taking food or

ii) Not drinking water at all.

This maxim describes the tendency of a frustrated man. When he is unsuccessful in obtaining something, consoles himself saying "Good,I did not get the thing. But actually I do not need that thing at all."

"Grapes are sour" to the fox which could not get the grapes even after many trials.

56. अभावविरक्तिन्यायः

This indirectly lays down the prohibition of not eating anything.

57. **अभ्यर्हितपूर्वन्यायः**

Ex. अभ्यर्हितं पूर्वमिति न्यायमाश्रत्यं तन्त्रप्रसङ्गप्रतिपादकथोरेकादश द्वादश द्वादशाध्यायोः पूर्वोत्तरभाव उपपादितःजैमिनीयन्यायमाला विस्तार-12

This maxim advises a man to mention first whatever is proper and desirable.

58. **अभ्युपगमसिद्धांतन्यायः**

Ex. अम्बुनि मज्जन्त्यलाबूनि, ग्रावाणः प्लवन्ते।

This maxim is applicable to the words which are blatantly false or directly against the facts.

59. **अभ्रमयूरन्यायः**

सदा मनोज्ञं स्तनदुत्सवोत्सुकं
विकीर्णविस्तीर्णकलापशोभितम्।
ससम्भ्रमालिङ्गनचुम्बनाकुलं
प्रवृत्तनृत्यं कुलमद्य बर्हिणाम्।। —ऋतुसंहार 2.6

The peacocks begin to dance on seeing the clouds in the rainy season. The mutual relation between the clouds and the peacocks is not clear. Similarly, a person is delighted on seeing another, though the reason is not apparent. This unknown cause of pleasure or happiness is what the maxim wants to speak about.

60. **अयस्कान्त (सूचि) न्यायः**

Example अयस्कान्तवद्रूपादिवच्च प्रवृतिरहिताप्त्वादपि प्रर्वतकादि।
—ब्रह्मसूत्रशङ्करभाष्य II.2.2

A magnet attracts an iron piece without actually doing anything. The puruṣa of the Sāmkhya philosophy makes the Prakṛti active without any action on his part. This maxim is applicable to a man who gets things done without doing anything. —सा० 919

61. **अयाचितमण्डलन्यायः**

Ex. **ईश्वरस्य सुहृदः स्वयं निर्धना अपि तदीयेन धनेन धन फलभाजस्तद्वत्।** —सा० 462

That which is obtained without any formal request is Ayācitaka. Many a time, the devotees are poor but they can achieve the fruit of the wealth by virtue of their devotion. This is what the maxim emphasizes on.

62. **अरण्यचन्द्रिकान्यायः**

निनिन्द रूपं हृदयेन पार्वती प्रियेषु सौभाग्य फला हि चारुता।
—कुमारसंभव 5.1; सा० 959

स्त्रीणां प्रियालोकफलो हि वेषः। —सुभाषितम्

Without the enjoyer or appreciator of the object of enjoyment alone is of no use. The maxim substantiates this idea by saying that the clear, cool, spread of moonlight in the forest is useless as there is nobody to enjoy or appreciate it.

63. **अरण्यरोदनन्यायः**

Cf. **अन्धदर्पणान्याय, उषटवृष्टिन्यायः**
अरण्यरुदितं कृतं शवशरीरमुद्वर्दितं
स्थले कमलरोपणं सुचिरमूषरे वर्षितम्।
श्वपुच्छमवनामितं बधिरकर्णजापः कृतः
कृतान्तमुखमण्डला यद्बुधौ जनः सेवितः।। —पञ्चतन्त्र 115

'Crying in the wilderness'. This maxim refers to the uselessness of crying in the wilderness,as that crying is not likely to arise sympathy in anybody. It conveys the idea of futile strain or the effort without getting any sympathy from anybody.

64. अरण्यामलकन्यायः

A myrbolon fruit (an Āmalakī fruit) is produced in some part of the forest. It is mixed with the salt which is produced in some part of the seashore. When these two are mixed together, it makes a good condiment. Similary, a man and a woman though born and brought up at different places, come together and lead a satisfactory and happy life. This maxim implies life as a whole.

65. अरुणान्यायः

Cf. जैमिनीसूत्र III 2.12; याज्ञवल्क्य III. 205

This maxim refers to a Mimāmsā arrangement. In one of the sentences in Taittiriya Samhitā, it is mentioned that a cow which is reddish, is one year old and has only one eye, should be exchanged for purchasing of Soma. It is established that when some attributes refer to one object and one injunction, it should be supported that all the attributes qualify one object only.

66. अरुन्धतीन्यायः

Ex. **यथाऽरुन्धतीं दिदर्शयिषुस्तत्समीपस्थां स्थूलांतारा ममुख्यां प्रथममरुन्धतीति ग्राहयित्वा तां प्रत्याख्यायपश्यादरुन्ध तीमेवग्राहयति, तद्वत् ब्रह्माणमत्मेति बृयात।**

—ब्रह्मसूत्र, शाङ्करभाष्य I.1-9

This maxim is concerned with the star Arundhati The bride and the bridegroom are asked to look at this star during their marriage. But some other star is shown at first which is easy to observe and then their attention is diverted to the exact Arundhati star. Thus a minor target is expected to be achieved before performing the main task.

67. अर्कमधुन्यायः

अर्के चेन्मधु विन्देत किमर्थं पर्वतां व्रजेत्।

This maxim tells that if someting can be obtained with less effort, one should not put forth rigorous efforts for securing that .If honey is available from a nearby Arka plant, one need not climb a high mountain to collect it or search for it in different places.

68. अर्धकुक्कुटीन्यायः

Cf. अर्धवैशसन्यायः

This maxim refers to a butcher who foolishly wanted to kill half part of the hen for eating and half of it for laying eggs. "One cannot eat the cake and have it too".

69. अर्धजरतीयन्यायः

Ex. विकारार्थे मयट्प्रवाहे सति आनन्दमय एवं कस्मादर्द्ध जरतीयन्यायेन कथमिव मयरः प्राचुर्यार्थत्वं ब्रह्मविषयत्वं वाश्रीयल इति। —ब्रह्मसूत्र, शाङ्करभाष्य 1.1.19 , 1.2.8

This maxim keeps in view an old lady whose husband loves her most. It is not that he loves her face only and hates her other limbs. It is not possible to discard some parts and accept some other parts of a person. So one should accept something or reject it in its entirety. For example, by following the Āgamas faithfully, one may reach God but by following the words of Buddha, one contradicts that.

70. अर्धवैशसन्यायः

Cf. अर्धजरतीयन्यायः, अर्धकुक्कुटीन्यायः **Example:—**

विधिना कृतमर्धवैशसं ननु मां कामवधे विमुञ्चता।
अनपायिनि संश्रयद्रुमे गजभग्ने पतनाय वल्लरी।।

—कुमारसम्भव, IV.31; सा० 876

Vaiśasa is killing. A hen can be killed for consumption or it may be preserved for getting its eggs. It cannot be killed in half and preserved in its half. Half killing is foolish or dangerous, as this maxim suggests.

71. अलातपिशाचन्यायः

When a firebrand is rotated, different circular figures are created. Some perceive these figures by rotating the firebrand as goblins or ghosts. But nobody has actually seen the goblin though much has been talked about them. This maxim is applicable to such false situations.

72. अलाबुपाषाणन्यायः

If a gourd is found inside a hard, thick rock, it will be as hard and thick as a rock. The company determines the qualities of a thing and shapes it accordingly.

73. अवटकच्छपन्यायः

Cf. कूपमण्डूकन्यायः

The maxim implies that the circumstances play a key role for changing the nature of a person. A man becomes broadminded or narrowminded according to the situation in which he is brought up, as a tortoise, living in a small puddle thinks that it is its world.

74. अवयवप्रसिद्धि-समुदायप्रसिद्धिन्यायः

Cf. जरामांसीन्यायः, रथन्तरन्यायः **Example** लब्धामिका हि समुदाय प्रसिद्धिरवयवप्रसिद्धिं बाधते। तस्यास्त्वात्मलाभो यत्र प्रमाणान्तरेण पूर्वानुभूतावयवरहितेऽर्थे शब्द प्रयोगो दृश्यते। यथा अश्वकर्णत्वरहिते वृक्ष अश्वकर्णशब्दस्य।

—तन्त्रवार्तिक I.4.11

If a compound (in Sanskrit language) is constituted of many words, having different meanings, the compound conveys meaning which might be different from the individual meanings of the constituent words. The constituted word conveys different meanings than those of the constituent words.

75. **अविरविकन्यायः**

The word Avi and Avika mean 'sheep.' But if the words are uttered consecutively, Avika means the flesh or the mutton of the sheep.

76. **अविवेकपुरोहितन्यायः**

At the time of the house-warming ceremony, the owner of the house requested the priest to find an auspicious Muhurta for the function. The son of the priest who was present there, saw the narrow door and immediately told the owner to make the door broad, considering the obesity of the mistress. His father-the priest frowningly said that if the wife gets stuck, the body can be cut into pieces and the door can be freed from obstruction.Needless to describe the reaction of the owner couple.

77. **अव्यापारेषुव्यापारोन्यायः**

Example : अव्यापारेषु व्यापार यो नरः कर्तुमिच्छति। स तत्र निर्धनं याति कीलोत्पाटीव वानरः। —हितोपदेश 2.30

The maxim refers to a person who does something of which he has no knowledge. He does those unnecessary things and ultimately is put to trouble. There is a famous story of a monkey which used to observe a carpenter working under the tree. When the carpenter left the place, this monkey began to imitate the woodcutter and unknowingly, by mistake, pulled out the piece of wood which was kept in the slit. Unluckily its testicles got stuck into the slit and it died. This is the result of doing things of which we are ignorant.

78. **अशोकवनिकान्यायः**

Why did Rāvaṇa keep Sitā in Aśokavana and not in any other place? There is no plausible answer to this question. Similarly a person does things according to his own choice though there are many alternative options before him. This is what the maxim suggests.

79. **अश्मलोष्टन्यायः** Cf. पाषाणेष्टकन्यायः

Ex. **गोपालपरशुरामौ उभावप्यतीब दुर्मेधसा।**
किन्तु अश्मलोष्टन्यायेन गोपालः परशुरामात् वरीयान्।

This maxim suggests that the clod of earth is harder than cotton but it is softer than a stone. Any quality is not absoute. It relatively exists in various objects.

80. **अश्वतरीगर्भन्यायः**

Ex. **सकृदुष्टमपीष्टं यः पुनः सन्धातुमिच्छति।**
समृत्युमुपगृह्णति गर्भमश्वतरी यथा।।

Cf. वृश्चिकीगर्भन्यायः कदलीफलन्यायः

A female horse and an ass, when united, give birth to a third type of animal called a 'mule.' But the female horse becomes the cause of its own death. The maxim suggests that he who tries to unite the desirable with the undesirable comes to ruin.

81. **अश्वत्थपत्रन्यायः**

As the leaves of the Peepal tree go on moving always, whether there is air or not, this maxim suggests that certain habits of a person never change. They last with him till his death.

82. अश्वभृत्यन्यायः

Cf. **बीजवृक्षन्यायः**

This maxim anticipates a peculiar conversation which does not result in any definite answer, as both horse and the servant are mutually dependent. One is the cause of the other.

83. असञ्जातविरोधन्यायः

The maxim refers to a person who is always haunted by the feeling of being opposed by somebody, though there is no opposition from any quarter in reality.

84. असिधाराव्रतन्यायः

This maxim refers to a situation which is as difficult as taking a vow of walking on a sword.

(i) It is told that observing detachment or celibacy for a man and a woman, sleeping on the same bed is as difficult as walking on a sharp blade of the sword.

(ii) This also refers to the most difficult observance of a vow which is as difficult as walking on the edge of a sword.

85. अस्त्रमस्त्रेणशाम्यतीतिन्यायः

Ex. नन्वस्त्रमस्त्रेण शाम्यति, इति न्यायेन काम्यैः काम्यानां निषिद्धैर्निषिद्धानां निवृत्तिरस्ति।

–नैष्कर्म्यसिद्धि, सुरेखरटीका

This maxim suggests the use of one missile, to prove another missile useless. The missile should be made stronger than the other one so that it becomes powerless.

86. अस्नेहदीपन्यायः

तत्र वर्षसहस्राणि निर्विकल्पसमाधिना।
दश स्थित्वा शशामासावात्मन्यस्नेहदीपवत्॥

–योगवासिष्ठ 2.1.44

A lamp burns till there is oil in it. When the oil is exhausted, it remains extinguished. It is a lamp for name's sake only. It does not serve the purpose of giving light.

87. अहिकुण्डलन्यायः

If one looks at a serpent, it appears to be one serpent only. But when one looks at it from distributive angles like its colour, coil, hood and the like, it appears with difference. It is one from the point of view of 'serpent-ness' but it appears in various forms, considering its hood, coil etc. The maxim has basis of the unitary and distributive point of view. The Brahman appears one, but when looked at from different point of view, it has multifarious forms.

88. अर्हिनकुलन्यायः

This maxim suggests the natural enmity between a serpent and a mungoose. Similarly, when there is natural enmity between two individuals, castes and communities, this maxim is applied.

89. अहिभुक्कैवर्तन्यायः

An intoxicated person sat in a boat and tied a thread to his leg as a mark of his identity. The boatman saw it and tied a thread to the leg of another traveller. When the boat arrived at the shore, the first traveller, still in the intoxicated mood, shouted "A person with the thread on his leg is myself". This suggests that an ignorant man forgets the real nature of himself and even declares that somebody else is himself only.

90. **आकाशमुष्टिहननन्यायः**

यस्तन्तूननुपादाय तुरीमात्रपरिग्रहात्।
पटं कर्तुं समहिते स हन्याद् व्योम मुष्टिभिः। –तन्त्र

Beating the firmament with the fists is doing something fruitlessly. That is the idea behind this maxim.

91. **आखुवन्नपिटकन्यायः** Cf. अशक्ता गृहनिर्माणे शक्तास्तु गृहभञ्जने

If a box, containing food is kept hanging, a mouse can pull it down. But it cannot lift up the fallen basket. Similarly, a wicked person can do some damage but cannot repair the damaged work.

92. **आदर्शगजन्यायः** Cf. हितोपदेश, विग्रह–12.

This maxim is a maxim of reflection. Even a big elephant can be seen in a mirror but only as a reflected one.

93. **आदर्शमलिनन्यायः**

A plain, clean mirror appears to be sullied by the dust deposited on it. The more clean and clear the mirror, the more it will appear soiled by the dust and dirt.

94. **आभाणकन्यायः**

"Abhaṇaka" is a saying or a proverb. The people are accustomed to cite an example saying "as it is said". They generally cite some adage which is current among the people.

95. **आमोदषट्पदन्यायः**

Ex. **अकारेणैव चतुरास्तर्कयन्ति परेङ्गितम्।**
गर्भस्थकेतकीपुष्पमामोदे नैव षट्पदाः॥

–सुभाषित रत्न भाण्डार, 158/233; सा० 781

Where there is fragrance, the bees swarm there to

enjoy it. So also, the appreciaters of the merit rush or gather there where there is merit.

96. आम्रवणन्यायः

Cf. मल्लग्रामन्यायः, ब्राह्मणन्यायः

There may be many different kinds of trees in a garden. But if there are some mango trees and these too in large number, the garden is known as a Mango grove, as the prominent things determine the nature of any collection.

97. आम्रसेकपितृतर्पणन्यायः

आम्राश्च सिक्ताः पितरश्च तृप्ताः।
एका क्रिया द्व्यर्थकरी प्रसिद्धा॥

—पातञ्जल महाभाष्य I.1.1.

This maxim refers to the advantages by doing one work. If one offers water to the manes near a mango tree and offers 'Tilānjali', two purposes are served. The mango tree gets water and the ancestors also are satisfied. It is like killing two birds with one stone.

98. आम्रान्पृष्टकोविदारानाचष्ट इति न्यायः

This maxim hints at a legend.

—महाभाष्य II.1.45; सा० 71

Once a man asked another person to describe a mango tree and where he could see that tree. But the other man instead of describing a mango tree, gave description of a 'Kovidāra' tree. The answer of this man created confusion in the mind of a person who asked him the question. This maxim suggests the irrelevant answers which create confusion in the mind of the person who puts the question.

99. आरघट्टघटीयन्त्रन्यायः

सार्धं घटीद्वयं नाडीरेकैकार्कोदयाद वहेत्।
आरघट्टघटीभ्रान्तिन्यायो नाड्योः पुनः पुनः॥

"Āraghaṭṭa" is a water-wheel, generally used for drawing water from the well. A pot tied to the rope is released in the well. When it is filled with water, it is drawn up, emptied and released again in the well. The air is inhaled by the nostrils, retained in the body for some moments and then it is exhaled. This process grows on unabatedly. The maxim shows the continuous repetition of the same act.

100. आरोहावरोहणन्यायः

The air in the body goes up through various plexuses—from Mulādhāra to Brahmarandhra—.This is Āroha. It comes back in the opposite direction. That is Avaroha. It is told that one should make the air reach in the uppermost Ājñācakra.

101. आशामोदकतृप्तन्यायः

आशामोदकतृप्ता ये ये चोपार्जितमोदकाः।
रसवीर्यविपाकादि तुल्यं तेषां प्रसज्जते॥ —न्यायकन्दली

A person may be immensely glad by eating imaginery sweets in the form of hopes. A man generally lives on hopes, thinking that the current bad days might pass away and the bright days may dawn. This maxim describes a person enjoying dreamy, imaginery joy.

102. इक्षुदण्डन्यायः

Every part of the sugarcane is sweet. The sweetness goes on increasing gradually from the top to the bottom. Similarly, friendship with the good persons also increases gradually.

103. इन्दुक्ष्वेडन्यायः

Śiva holds Ganga on his head and poison in the throat. Likewise, a wise and intelligent man accepts both merits and faults. He appreciates the virtues of others and ignores their faults. As Śiva conceals the poison in the throat and holds Ganga in a prominent position, a good man conceals the defects and displays the virtues of others.

104. इन्द्रजालन्यायः

Ex. एतस्मात् किमितेन्द्रजालनपरं यद्गर्भवासस्थितं
रेतश्चेतति हस्तमस्तकपदप्रोदभूतनानाङ्कुरम्।
पर्याये शिशुवयौवनजरावेषैरनेकैर्वृतं
पश्यत्यत्ति शृणोति जिध्रति तथाऽगच्छत्ययो गच्छति॥

Indrajāla means a magical net. It also means a skilful method by which one thing is shown to be different. It is incomprehensible how a magician changes one thing into some other thing. Like wise, even the life of a man is also mystical and incomprehensible, right from his birth upto his death.

105. इषुकारन्यायः

A craftsman who manufactures arrows, is much engrossed in doing his work. He does not notice anything what is going on around him or who is coming and who is going. This maxim hints at such one-pointed enrapt attention in any work.

106. इषुवेगक्षयन्यायः

The arrow which is shot with great speed at the beginning, gets its speed reduced gradually. Similarly a man starts to do some work energetically but his enthusiasm decreases gradually. The maxim tells that the initial force or application of a man goes on decreasing as time passes off.

107. उत्खातदंष्ट्रोरगन्यायः

When the poisonous fang of a serpent is removed, the serpent cannot bite a person. Even if it tries to bite, it is of no use. It becomes useless. The maxim tells that if certain powerful limb of a person becomes useless, he cannot perform his duties in the proper manner. When that limb is cut off, it is useless like the slough of the serpent.

108. उदकनिमज्जनन्यायः

Cf. विषभक्षणन्यायः, घटारोहणनयायः, तप्तमाक्षिकोद्धरणन्यायः

Water drunk in a limited quantity, quenches the thirst of a person. But when he thinks that there is plenty of water in a reservoir or a pond, he jumps into it. Then that water becomes his killer. The maxim tells that limited use of anything may be beneficial but use of it in excessive quantity becomes fatally dangerous.

109. उदके (उदक) विशीर्ण इति न्यायः

Water and fire are useful in their own separate existence. If fire is thrown in water or if water is sprinkled on fire, both ways the fire extinguishes and the water evaporates. When fire and water are brought near each other, they see their own end. This maxim envisages fruitless or useless work. (like bringing hostile elements together).

110. उद्योगराघवन्यायः

Rāma had resolved to discover Sītā and bring about the end of Rāvaṇa. On knowing his pious intention, all the semi-gods and even the monkeys extended their helping hands. Rāma had undertaken a noble task of killing Rāvaṇa and the Rākṣasas. So all the gods supported him.

111. उपसर्गन्यायः

उपसर्गेण धात्वर्थो बलादन्यत्र नीयते।
प्रहाराहारसंहारविहारपरिहारवत्॥

In Sanskrit, there are some prefixes which are placed before the roots. When the prefix is fixed before the original root, it often causes some change in the meaning of the root. This maxim envisages that situation in which many imports are expected from one object.

112. उभयतस्पाशरज्जुन्यायः

Ex. यद्यपि न बोधस्तथापि विकल्पस्तावत् प्राप्नोति।
न हि तुल्यार्थानां क्वाचत् समुच्चयो दृष्टः।
सेयमुभयस्तस्पाशा रज्जुः। —तन्त्रवार्तिक III.6.42

अभावः कारणमेव न भवतीति चेत्
तदा वक्तव्यमभावस्य कार्यत्वमस्ति न वा।
यदि नास्ति तदा घटप्रध्वसानुत्पत्त्या घटस्य नित्यताप्रसङ्गः।
अथास्ति किमपराद्ध कारणत्वमेवेति सेयमुभयतस्पाशा रज्जुः।

—सर्वदर्शनसंग्रहः, बौद्धप्रकरण, पृ० 282

Fetters on one side and a rope on the other. One rope can fasten a thing from both its ends. It leads to an impasse between the two horns of a dilemma. This maxim underlines that situation of impasse.

113. उलूखलमुसलन्यायः

This maxim refers to an imaginery conversation between a mortar and a pestle. The mortar went to a pestle and complained that it is being beaten always. The pestle, in turn, complained that it receives strokes from both the sides. The maxin suggests that everybody suffers in life but he carries an impression that he suffers heavily, more than anybody else.

114. उष्ट्रकण्टकभक्षणन्यायः

Ex. **कर्णामृतं सूक्तिरसं विमुच्य दोषेषु यत्नः सुमहान् खलस्य।**
अवेक्षते केलिवनं प्रविश्य क्रमेलकः कण्टकजालमेव॥

—विक्रम० I.4

A camel eats the leaves of the thorny trees. Even though he is left in a beautiful garden, he searches for the thorny tree and eats the leaves of that tree only. In the society also, the wicked persons take pleasure in pointing out the faults of others. The maxim suggests that nothing is painful or delightful by itself. Everybody does not like everything. There is subjective element in all likes and dislikes.

115. उष्ट्रलगुडन्यायः

अयं हि स्वमते परेणोद्भाव्यमानानां दूषणानां तन्मते पातनेऽवतरति। —लौ० न्यायः

A person puts some load on the back of a camel and continues his journey. Sometimes he puts a stick on the loaded matter. The camel carries that stick also. But if the occasion arises, the owner hits it with it. A rival may use the arguments already advanced by the disputant against him also.

116. उष्ट्रशूलन्यायः

If a camel suffers from the stomache-ache, what should be done ? What is the remedy? ?Which medicine should be given? Nothing much. Take a big pestle and beat the camel with it. Everything becomes all right. This applies to a man also. The maxim tells that a man can be brought to book by thrashing.

117. उषरबीजन्यायः

If a seed is sown on a barren land, it will not germinate, eventhough the land receives heavy rains. The maxim can be extended to human beings also. A man lacking good Samskāras, does not show any good results.

118. उषरवृष्टिन्यायः

Even though showers of heavy rain fall on the barren and salty land, nothing can grow on such a land. It does not serve any purpose of germinating the seed on this unfertile land. Similarly, even if many facilities are provided to a dull-witted student, they are of no use. Such a student will not increase his knowledge despite giving him all kinds of facilities.

119. उर्णनाभिन्यायः

A spider spreads a net with the help of some sticky substance and unwinds it in the same manner. The Almighty also, creates the world through his own Self and withdraws it in his own body. The maxim tells us that creation and dissolution of this world take place exactly like the mode or fashion of the spider.

120. ऊहापोहन्यायः

Ūha is inference and Apoha is setting aside, removing Any polemic dispute proceeds on the two prongs. This procedure is the very disputation itself, as the maxim indicates. —सा० 920

121. ऋतुमतीकन्यकान्यायः

In olden days. the marriage preparations used to start when the girl used to attain the age of puberty. After the marriage, she used to go to her husbandś house, leaving the house of her parents. She thus used to get a long lasting support.

122. ऋतुलिङ्गन्यायः

A particulars verse related to the seasons occurs in many works. The verse is as follows—

यथार्तावृतुलिङ्गानि नानारूपाणि पर्यये।
दृश्यन्ते तानि तान्येव, यथा भावा युगदिषु॥

—महाभारत, शान्ति० 233.15; तन्त्रवार्तिक 1.37; वेदान्तसूत्र 1.3.30; वायुपुराण 9.65; विष्णुपुराण 1.5.61.

123. एकदेशाविकृतन्यायः

Even if a tail or an ear of a dog is cut off, the dog remains a dog only. If a limb of a man is broken, he remains the same. His original nature remains unchanged.

124. एकपुत्रन्यायः

(i) **वरमेको गुणी पुत्रो न च मूर्खशतान्यपि।**
एकश्चन्द्रस्तमो हन्ति न च तारागणोऽपि च॥

(ii) **एकेनापि सुपुत्रेण सिंही स्वपिति निर्भयम्।**
सदैव दशभिः पुत्रर्भारं वहति रासभी॥

—सुभाषितरत्नभाण्डागार 6,7/90.

It is better to have one good, meritorious, virtuous son than having hundreds of bad, wicked and unrighteous sons. It is the virtue or the good behaviour which makes a man strong and popular in society and not the physical number.

125. एकवृन्तगतफलद्वयन्यायः

इह हि सभङ्गश्लेषस्य शब्दद्वयवृत्तित्वं जतुकाष्ठन्यायेन, अभङ्गस्य चार्थद्वयवृत्तित्वमेकवृन्तगतफलद्वयवच्च स्फुटमेव।

—रसगङ्गाधर, पृ० 536

One stem of a tree sometimes, bears two fruits at a time. This maxim indicates the achievement of many results, through one action only. The famous figure of speech 'Sleṣa' (paranomasia) is actually conveyed poetically. It conveys more than one meaning of one word.

126. एरण्डबीजन्यायः

The castor seed slips off from the tree. But it rises up and gets stuck up to the tree again. Similarly, a man attain good state and prosperity when he becomes free from the worldly chains. —सा० 705

127. कटकगवोदाहरणन्यायः

Once a cowherd came to know that no arrangement was made for the protection of the cows. So he constructed a closed enclosure and kept all his cows inside it. Once the enclosure caught fire and all the cows were burnt in it. This maxim, based on this anecdote, conveys that despite safe guards, fate becomes uncertain. What a man proposes, fate may dispose it off. Despite one's utmost efforts. fate may undo one's efforts.

128. कण्टकन्यायः

The word "Kanṭaka" has atleast two meanings. One is 'a thorn' and other is 'an enemy.' If one is pricked by a thorn, one tries to remove it with the thorn to avoid further trouble. Similarly, one tries to crush one's enemy with the help of other enemy and then tries to ruin the other enemy. This is the stratagem on which this maxim is based.

129. कण्ठचामीकरन्यायः

प्रत्यगात्मतया तस्य प्राप्तत्वेऽपिच सर्वदा।
कण्ठचामीकरन्यायात् तत्प्राप्तिरुपचर्यते॥

'Cāmīkara' means gold. Secondarily any golden ornament is called Cāmīkara! It also means golden chain put around the neck. A stupid person has no idea about the golden chain, he has put on. Similarly, a person, though Brahman from the ultimate point of view, does not realize it, owing to ignorance only. A teacher can make him realize it. Though Brahman is indirectly realized through understanding, the real nature of the individual soul; the self as it were is not realized owing to the influence of Māyā. It is the advice of the preceptor which advises him to realize it inwardly.

130. कतकरेणुन्यायः

This maxim is generally applied to a person who wipes off the bad qualities of other person just by his contact,as the fruit called 'Kataka' removes the dirt from the water when that fruit is put in it.

131. कदम्बगोलकन्यायः

पित्रा स्वपाणिपद्मेन स्पृश्यमानोऽवनिपतिः।
उत्कोरकदम्बाभौ बभूव पुलकाङ्कुरैः।

—हेमचन्द्र परिशिष्टपर्य 1.24

वीचीतरङ्गन्यायेन तदुत्पत्तिस्तु कीर्तिता।
कदम्बकोरकन्यायादुत्पत्तिः कस्यचिन्मते।।

—जयन्त, न्यायमञ्जरी, पृ० 214, 228

The Kadamba tree puts forth buds simultaneously. This maxim is applied to a situation when many events occur simultaneously.

132. कदलीकण्टकन्यायः

Whether a thorn gets stuck up to a plantain tree or a plantain tree is pierced by the thorn, the result is the same! Both ways, the plantain tree only suffers.

Similarly, when a good person comes in contact with a wicked person, a good person only suffers and not the bad person. This is the import of the maxim.

133. कनककुण्डलन्यायः

Ex. वाचारम्भणं विकारो नामधेयं सुवर्णमित्येव सत्यम्।

Gold and golden ornaments are the same from the point of view of 'being gold', though they are different in shape. This maxim shows the essential unity between cause and effect. Accordingly, the world is the effect which is not different from the Brahman which is the cause.

134. कन्दुकन्यायः

A ball when pressed down with force, jumps up, as it is its nature. It does not get pressed even though we apply full force on it. Following this, the maxim suggests that even if a good man is suppressed or denigrated, he is not affected by it. He attains his original position by his good and virtuous deeds.

135. कपिञ्जलन्यायः

There is an injunction in the Brāhmaṇas that the Kapiñjala birds should be sacrificed but the number of these birds is not mentioned. This doubt arises because the word Kapiñjala is used in plural. So it can be inferred that at least three birds should be killed. This maxim is applied to those items where the grammatical form determines the meaning of the word.

—जैमिनिसूत्र 11.1.38-46

136. कपित्थभंगन्यायः

जानन्नपि खलु जातिं तव न जानामि शीलविभवेन।
तिष्ठतु ममैव मनसि किं कपित्थेन भग्नेन।।

—मृच्छकटिक 6.21

Even if a wood-apple fruit is broken, it does not yield any substantial matter, as it is almost hollow inside. Too much of analysis leads to disappointment.

This maxim is used in the Sanskrit drama "Mṛchha kaṭika". considering the caste of somebody is as useless as breaking the wood-apple fruit.

137. कफोणिगुडन्यायः

This maxim suggests two meanings.

(i) To ask somebody to lick the jaggery, kept on his elbow which is impossible,

(ii) To act or pretend the licking of jaggery, even though it is not actually placed on the elbow.

138. कमठीदुग्धन्यायः

This maxim is applied to those futile cases like the milk of a female tortoise which cannot even be imagined as drinkable.

139. कम्बलनिर्णेजनन्यायः

निर्णेजनं ह्युभयं करोति कम्बलशुद्धिं पादयोश्च निर्मलताम्।

—शाबरभाष्य, जैमिनि 2.25

While washing a blanket, even the feet of the washerman are washed or cleaned. This maxim is applied to the situation in which two works are accomplished at a time.

140. करकङ्कणन्यायः

(I) The word "Karakankaṇa" the word kara is redundant. Even the word karakankaṇa is in currency, probably suggesting that the bracelet is worn on the wrist and not placed in the ornament-box.

141. करटदन्तन्यायः

Counting the teeth of the crow is a useless endeavour. This maxim is applied for wasting time in doing such a useless task.

142. करदीपिकान्यायः

This maxim suggests that if one has got a lamp in one's hand, it becomes useful to oneself as well as to others also.

143. करबदरन्यायः

A Badari fruit in the hand is clearly visible. This maxim applies to those things which are clearly visible or distinct.

144. करभदोहदन्यायः

If we have a cow which yields milk, why should we try to milch a female camel or a female ass? This maxim suggests that when excellent devices are available, one should not think of using ordinary devices.

145. करभपृष्ठकण्ठन्यायः

A camel is known as a beast of burden. It carries huge luggage on its back. But the things which cannot be put on its back, are put around its neck. It has to carry huge burden which is inevitable, a beast of burdon has to suffer.

146. करिकलभन्यायः

When the word 'kalabha' is used, it means a young one of an elephant. The word 'Kari' in 'karikalabha' is redundant. Such redundant usages are frequently found in the language. But there is no necessity of this kind of usage. However, sometimes some reason can be assigned to such redundants.

147. करिघण्टान्यायः

मतिरेव बलाद् गरीयसी यदभावे करिणामियं दशा।
इति घोषयतीव डिण्डिमः करिणो हस्तिपकाहतः क्वणन्॥

—गुणरत्न 8; सा० 653

It is difficult to control an intoxicated elephant. It can move anywhere and crush anything which comes in its way. In order to ward the people off from this intoxicated elephant, a bell is tied around its neck. This maxim suggests that intelligence is superior to strength. In the absence of which the elephants´are completely dependent on the driver. Despite its strength, the intelligent driver can control the elephant. So intelligence is superior to strength.

148. करिणीप्रसवन्यायः

A female pig gives birth to many young ones at a time but the female elephant gives birth to only one cub. Even then the elephant is superior to the pig qualitatively though not quantitatively.

149. करिबृंहितन्यायः

Cf—गजघटान्याय, नीलेन्दीवरन्याय, पर्वताधित्यकान्याय, वाजिमन्दुरान्याय, मृगवागुरान्याय इ०

विशिष्टवाचकानामपि पदानां सति पृथग्विशेषणवाचक पदसमवधाने विशेष्यमात्रपरतायां करिवृहितन्यायः प्रवर्तते।

—लौकिकन्याय साहस्रीतः, उद्धृतं—रघुनाथ

The word'Bṛṁhita' means the trumpeting of an elephant. The word 'kari' is redundant. The prefixed word may indicate some speciality of trumpeting. There are many adages or maxims like this.

150. कर्कटीगर्भन्यायः

When karkaṭī tree bears fruit, it also bears some other

types of fruit. As soon as those fruits appear, the original, genuine fruits are destroyed. The maxim is used to describe a situation in which sundry things survive and the chief matter is ruined.

151. **कर्णकौन्तेयन्यायः**

Cf. **राजपुत्रव्याधन्यायः**

So long as Karṇa did not know that he was the son of Kuntī, he was thinking that he was the son of Rādhā. When he came to know the truth, he began to call himself the son of Kuntī. This maxim is used when the later realization (reality) dawns on a person.

152. **कर्मविपर्यासन्यायः**

This maxim is applicable to a situation in which the order of cause and effect is reversed.

153. **कलविङ्कघटन्यायः I यथा घटेवरुद्धः कलाविङ्कस्तन्मुखापावरणे बहिरुड्डीय गच्छति, तर्हितकल्पनापि सत्या।**

—योगवासिष्ठ, निर्वाण, उत्तरार्ध 97.10

The Kalavinka bird which is caught in a closed earthen pot, flies away as soon as the cover of the pot is removed. So also the individual soul encased in the body, escapes immediately when the actions (and their effects) are annihilated.

154. **कलविङ्कघटन्यायः II**

कलविङ्कघटन्यायो धर्म इत्यपि तद्विदाम्।
तथात्मसिद्धे म्लेच्छानां तद्देशेषु न दुष्यति।

—योगवासिष्ठ, निर्वाण, उत्तरार्ध 97-10

If a Kalavinka bird is kept in a jar, closed with a lid and after some time the lid is removed, the bird inside soon escapes. Similarly, the individual self encased in a body, becomes free when the body falls down. The Yogavāsiṣṭḥa text refers to this maxim.

155. **काकतालीयन्यायः**

Ex. **तालः करतलयोः शब्दजनकः संयोगः। तस्मिन् क्रियमाणे उत्पतन् काको दैवात् तत्र तालाभ्यामाक्रान्तोऽभूत्। तदेतत् काकतालीयमुच्यते।**

—नीलकण्ठटीका, महाभारत, शान्ति० 12.17.11.

If a crow perches on the branch of a Tāla (palmyra)tree it breaks. It does not give way owing to the weight of the crow. As such, the maxim describes the events which take place casually or by coincidence. Various explanations are given about the relation of the crow and the branch of the Tāla tree.

156. **काकत्रोटिबिम्बन्यायः**

A crow imagines that its beak is the Bimba fruit. This maxim denotes a person who is ignorant about himself.

157. **काकदन्तगवेषणन्यायः**

Ex. (i) **पञ्चपादिका, पृ० 53-68**

(ii) **जयन्त न्यायमञ्जरी, पृ० 7**

नचिकेतो मरणं मरण सम्बन्धं प्रश्नं प्रेत्यास्तीति नास्तीति काकदन्तपरीक्षारूपं मानुप्राक्षीर्मैवं वक्तुमर्हसि।

—शाङ्करभाष्यं, कठोपनिषद् 1.25

Finding out or counting the teeth of a crow is an impossible task. It is a waste of time in doing such a useless work. This sense of useless task and wasting our precious time in doing fruitless work is conveyed by this maxim.

158. **काकदध्युपघातन्यायः**

A person who was going out, asked the person who

was at home to protect the curds from the crow. This actually implies that the person should prōlect it from various dangers. But this person followed the advice literally. He protected it from the crows but allowed the dog to gulp the curd.. 'kāka' is the representative (Upalakṣaṇa) of all such animals which spoil the curds. But this stupid fellow didnot understand it. The maxim points to such a thoughtless person.

159. काकपिकन्यायः

Cf. काचमणिन्यायः

काकः कृष्णः पिकः कृष्णः को भेदः पिककाकयोः।
वसन्तसमये प्राप्ते काकः काकः पिकः पिकः॥

A crow and a cuckoo both-are black in comprehension. But there is a vast difference in their qualities. The maxim shows the difference between two persons, though they may appear similar apparently. The difference between a crow and a cuckoo is visible clearly in the 'Vasant' season i.e. (spring season).

160. काकरुतभीरुन्यायः

Once an affectionate and a loving couple was enjoying sound sleep. Suddenly the beloved heard the harsh crowing of a crow. Being alarmed, she embraced her husband firmly. Actually this lady was not a coward because she had come to her lover after crossing the river Narmadā, a few hours ago. The maxim suggests that one may venture to do something. After achieving that one is likely to submit oneself to ones own instincts like fear.

161. काकवन्ध्यान्यायः

It is believed that the eggs of a female cuckoo are hatched by a crow. As the female crow does not hatch its eggs, it always feels that it is barren. It does not get its own progeny. A woman whose children die immediately after their birth, is called 'Kākavandhyā'.

162. काकाक्षिगोलकन्यायः

Example बलिनोद्विषतोर्मध्ये वाचात्मानं समर्पयन्।
द्वैधीभावेन वर्तेत काकाक्षिवदलक्षितः॥
अविरोधिसुखे बुद्धिः स्वानन्दे च गमागमौ।
कुर्वन्त्यास्ते क्रमादेषा काकाक्षिवदितस्ततः॥
एकैव दृष्टिः काकस्य वामदक्षिणनेत्रयोः।
यात्यायात्येवमानन्दद्वये तत्त्वविदो मतिः॥
—जैमिनिसूत्र, तन्त्रवार्तिक, 6.2.1

This maxim speaks about the pupil of the eye of a crow. A crow can see with one eye only and turns that eye towards the things to be perceived. The maxim is utilized to explain the formation of the word 'Antarīpa' in Amarkośa. The word 'Dvīpa' is in both the genders —masculine and Neuter, so is the word Antarīpa.

163. काकाधिकरणन्यायः

When a person was asked. "Which is Devadatta'ś house?", He replied "That house on which the crow is perching". But perching of a crow cannot be taken to be an exclusive characteristic of a house. This maxim is applied to a statement which furnishes imperfect proof.

164. काकिणीन्यायः

The maxim indicates quarrels which are caused by money. —Kākiṇi

165. काकोलूकनिशान्यायः

पत्रं नैव यदा करीरविटपे दोषो वसन्तस्य किं नोलूकोऽप्यवलोकते यदि दिवा सूर्यस्य कि दूषणम्।

The brightness of the day is the morning time for a crow but it is night for an owl, as it cannot see anything in the day time. The time for visibility for both of them is different. This maxim points out that the natural characteristics of a being cannot be changed.

166. काचकुम्भद्वीपन्यायः

The glass cover over the burning wick of a lamp acts as its protector. Even the strong wind of a storm cannot extinguish it. This maxim suggests that there need not be any fear or danger when adequate protection is provided.

167. काचमणिन्यायः

Ex. मणिर्लुठति पादेषु काचः शिरसि धार्यते।
क्रयविक्रयवेलायां काचः काचो मणिर्मणिः।

A jewel and a piece of glass appear to be alike. But there is a vast difference in their properties. The worth of a thing is determined by its inner qualities and not by its external appearance.

168. कान्तारन्यायः

Two travellers were travelling separately. After some time, they came near a forest. They were afraid of enter king the forest. So both of them came together and jointly began to discover the route. After crossing over the dangerous route of the jungle, they began to travel separately and took separate courses. It is the need which makes people friends for a limited time. Once the need is over, the friendship also wanes away.

169. काशकुशावलम्बनन्यायः

Ex. (i) सर्वदर्शन सङ्ग्रह, आर्हत दर्शन, पृ० 21.

(ii) नैष्कर्म्यं सिद्धि I.76.

(iii) तन्त्रवार्तिक I.3.8.

A drowning man tries hard to save himself by catching whatever comes at hand in the water. He tries to hold even a blade of grass forgetting that it can not be a proper support to save him: He tries hectically to save himself from drowning.

170. कांस्यभोजन न्यायः

This maxim refers to the custom of taking food in a plate, made of white copper or bell-metal. A disciple determines to eat food, left over by the teacher in a bell-metal plate. The teacher also began to take food in such a plate, though it was not compulsory for the teacher to take food in that plate. The teacher was particular to see that the vow of the pupil is not violated.

171. कीटभृङ्गन्यायः

If a bee catches an insect , it becomes so much panic. stricken that it begins to think about the danger from the bee, day and night. It thinks so much about it that the insect becomes the bee itself. This maxim refers to the deepest type of meditation.

172. कीटोद्धारन्यायः

This maxim refers to a person, striving hard to save his life, as an insect thrown out from the running water, takes resort on a tree somehow or other.

173. कीलप्रतिकीलन्यायः

Two nails hold fast a wheel firmly. Similarly the act of advancing strong arguments establish some doctrine firmly.

174. कुक्कुटध्वानन्यायः

This maxim refers to a gradually increasing or growing matter which is like the sound, coming from a cock.

The sound of the cock is weak in the beginning but goes on increasing slowly.

175. कुण्डधारोपास्तिन्यायः

Once a person served a Yakṣa called Kuṇḍadhara sincerely. As the Yakṣa didnot have the power to give a boon, he managed to give a boon to the devotee from the deity. The good persons, in spite of their weakness, try to do good to the people through somebody. The good people try to increase the Sattva quality of a man when they want to help. The maxim underlines this trait of the character of good men.

176. कुमारीकङ्कणन्यायः

This maxim refers to a legend when some persons came to a certain house to see a girl. They heard the noise of the bangles when the girl started pounding. The bangles slowly dropped except one and the noise practically stopped. This legend suggests that a person alone can attain peace by meditation without the assistance of anybody else.

177. कुमारीकङ्कणन्यायः

बहूनां कलहो नित्यं द्वाभ्यां सङ्घर्षणं तथा।
एकाकी विचरिष्यामि कुमारीकङ्कणं यथा॥

A man who tries to have company with many, may not be happy, as the company with many may result in quarrels, Even the company of one cannot avoid differences. One bracelet on the wrist of a virgin lady does not create any sound. So the man ultimately decides to live without the company of anybody else.

178. कुम्भदीपिकान्यायः

A lamp which is burning inside a jar, may not be seen

from outside but it continues to burn inside. So also, the maxim assumes, the brilliance of a man may not be seen externally, nevertheless, it does exist internally.

179. कुम्भीधान्यन्यायः

'Kumbhī' is a container in which grains are stored. If an injunction says that a cow should be presented to a Brāhmaṇa who has stored grains in kumbhī. 'Kumbhī' has no particular singificance, as grains are generally stored in a container only. In order to avoid the fruitless nature of the word, the compound can be dissolved as Brāhmaṇa having grains in one kumbhi only, indicating his poverty.

180. कुलकन्यकान्यायः

Ex. सत्यं सन्ति गृहे गृहे सुकवयो येषां वचश्चातुरी
स्वे हर्म्ये कुलकन्यकेव लभते जातैर्गुणैर्गौरवम्।

A woman, having beauty, quality and character gets due respect in her mother's house only. Inspite of having many good qualities, she has to work hard in her inlaw's house and does not get proper respect in her husband's house.Even then she cannot stay for a long period in her mother's house because her proper place is in her husband's house and the people in the society also give respect only when she remains in her mother-in law's house.

181. कुलालचक्रन्यायः

A potter rotates his wheel speedily with the help of a stick in his hand. Even though he withdraws his hand and the stick from the wheel, the rotation continues for some time. The maxim, based on this event of the potter's wheel, tells that the impressions of good behaviour and virtuous character of a person do not disappear. —सा० 702

182. कुलालचक्रकीटन्यायः

Ex. यथा कुलालचक्रेण भ्रमता सह भ्रमतां तदाश्रयाणां पिपीलिकादीनां गतिरन्यैव प्रदेशान्तरेष्वप्युपलभ्यमानत्वादेवं नक्षत्रराशिभिरूपलक्षितेन कालचक्रेण ध्रुवं मेरुंच प्रदक्षिणेन परिधावता सह परिधावमानानां तदाश्रयाणां सूर्यादीनां ग्रहाणां गतिरन्यैव नक्षत्रान्तरे राश्यन्तरे चोपलभ्यमानत्वात्। —सा० 597

This maxim indirectly refers to a verse in the Bhāgavata Purāṇa. The potter's wheel moves in a particular direction. If something is placed on the wheel, it appears to be moving in the opposite direction. The small insects, like ants,appear to be rotating in a different way. The mountains like Meru and the planets like. Dhruva and also the movement of the sun, moving in conconance with the time wheel, appear to be different.

183. कुल्याप्रणयनन्यायः

This maxim suggests that one act may yield many fruits, giving the example of the water of the canal which is useful not only to the fields but also for drinking and for many other purposes too.

184. कुशकाशावलम्बनन्यायः

Kuśa is a type of grass and kāśa also is a type of grass which has white flowers. Both kuśa and kāśa are very thin and weak type of plants and it is dangerous to catch hold for rescue in times of danger. The maxim points at a man who advances feeble arguments or takes support of weak things.

185. कुसुमस्तबकन्यायः

Ex. कुसुमस्तबकस्येव द्वे वृत्ती तु मनस्विनाम्।
मूर्ध्नि वा सर्वलोकस्य विशीर्येत वनेऽथवा।।
—भर्तृहरि, नीतिशतक, 33

A bunch of flowers has two positions generally. These flowers either adore the head and other parts of the body of a human being or they are placed on the dead bodies as a mark of respect and they fade away. Similarly, the men of self-respect are highly respected in the society or fade out unheard and unsung.

186. कुसूलधान्यन्यायः

Ex. विष्टभ्याहमिदं कृत्स्नमेकांशेन स्थितो जगत्।

—नीलकंठ

The store- houses of grains are full with grains generally. They are completely rich with grains. The maxim applies to a person who is rich and perfect in all respect, like the store-houses which are completely filled with grains.

187. कूटकार्षापणन्यायः

Ex. शब्दापभ्रंशवदेव गौणभ्रान्त्यादिप्रयोगनिमित्ता अर्थापभ्रंशा भवन्ति, ते शास्त्रस्थैरेवाविप्लुतार्थ क्रियानिमित्तपुण्यर्षिभिः शक्यन्ते, साध्वसाधुकार्षापणमध्यादिव तत्परीक्षिभिर्विवेक्तुम्।

—तन्त्रवार्तिक, 1.3.8

If a faked coin is in currency, it should be withdrawn from circulation as early as possible. On the same line, the maxim tells that the Smṛtis which go against the Śrutī should be discarded immediately.

188. कूपकूर्मन्यायः

Cf. **कूपमण्डूकन्यायः**

A tortoise, living in a well, thinks that the well in which it is living, is the only world around it. Narrow-minded person thinks that the world around him is the entire world. The maxim also suggests that a person accustomed to live in a small circle, does not feel like giving it up like the tortoise in the well.

189. कूपकूखननन्यायः

The maxim depicts a man who thinks of digging a well when his house is blazing with fire or when he feels thirsty suggesting, thereby, the nature of a man who does not provide anything for the future or for probable difficulties and runs hither and thither for help in the time of difficulty.

190. कूपखानकन्यायः

Cf. कूपकूर्मन्यायः यावत्स्वस्यमिदं शरीरमरुतं यावज्जरा दूरतो
यावच्चेन्द्रियशक्तिरप्रतिहताः यावत्क्षयो नायुषः।
आभिश्रेयसि तावदेव विदुषा कार्यः प्रयत्नो मशन्
सन्दीप्ते भवने तु कूपखननं प्रत्युद्यमः कीदृशः॥

—भर्तृहरि, नीतिशतक 138

When a person digs a well, some water and mud bound to fall on his body, spoiling his clothes and body. But after some time of digging, fresh water starts flowing from the well. He cleans his clothes and body with the same clean, fresh water. Similarly, the faults engendered by the dualistic attitude, are cleared off by developing Advaita or monistic spirit.

191. कूपमण्डूकन्यायः Cf. कूपकूर्मन्यायः

A frog moves about in a well. It does not go out of that limited area. So it thinks that the well around it is the only real world. This maxim describes a person who is narrow minded.

192. कूपयन्त्रघटीन्यायः

Ex. काँश्त्तिुच्छयति प्रपूरयति वा काँश्चिन्नयत्युन्नतिं
काँश्चित् पातविधौ करोति च पुनःकाँश्चिन्नयत्याकुलान्।

अन्योन्यं प्रतिपक्षसन्ततिमिमां लोकस्थितिं बोधय-
न्नेष क्रीडति कूपयन्त्रघटिकान्याय प्रसंक्तो विधिः॥

—मृच्छकटिक, 10.59; सा० 664

In a contrivance at a well, on a rotating wheel with many pitchers are attached to it. As the wheel goes down, the jars are filled with water. When they come up along with the wheel, they are emptied. Again they go below and come up. Thus the wheel goes on filling and emptying the jars. The fate or providence also rotates like a wheel, changing the fortunes of human beings. This is what a verse in Mṛcchakaṭika tells us.

It empties or fills up some; it elevates some and (degrades some) makes some fall down and makes some anxious, (thus) making (all) realize this state of things in the world—conveying the sense of the maxim "the well machine and the buckets".

193. कूर्मकिशोरन्यायः

The maxim is a reflection on a man of forgetful nature, who is compared to a female tortoise. The she-tortoise has a forgetful nature. She forgets that she has laid eggs. Suddenly she remembers and tries to find the place where she had laid the eggs. This is how the man of a forgetful nature is described.

194. कूर्माङ्गन्यायः

(i) वाचस्पति मिश्र साङ्ख्यतत्त्वकौमुदी कारिका-9.18.

(ii) मुण्डकोपनिषद्-3.

(iii) भगवद्गीता-2.68.

Ex. **यदा संहरते चायं कर्मोऽङ्गानीव सर्वशः।**
इंद्रियाणि इंद्रियार्थेभ्यस्तस्य प्रज्ञा प्रतिष्ठिता॥

—भगवद्गीता 2.58.

A tortoise has the skill (knack) of withdrawing its limbs under its broad, hard, thick back when it senses some danger. The limbs when withdrawn, are not seen apparently. Similarly, when the effect-matter becomes apparent, the casual matter remains unseen. When the effect matter is destroyed, it becomes one with the causal matter.

195. कृतक्षौरनक्षत्रपरीक्षान्यायः

मुण्डितशिरोनक्षत्रान्वेषणम्, कृते कार्ये किं मुहूर्तप्रश्नेन। न हि विवाहानन्तरं वरपरीक्षा।

In the olden days, an auspicious day was fixed for doing the first hair-cut. Even in modern days also, this custom of finding an auspicious good day for doing birth hair-cut prevails. But this indication of finding a lucky, auspicious star should be obviously considered before the actual shaving otherwise that ascertaining of the auspicious star will be purposeless after the actual hair cutting as the merits and demerit of the bridegroom should be considered before the actual marriage takes place. It is useless afterwards.

196. कृतप्रणाशाकृताभ्यागमप्रसङ्गन्यायः

The maxim states two things—accepting those meritorious deeds which are not actually performed, as fruit bearers and accepting the loss of the (fruits of) actions done.

197. कृपणधन न्यायः

Ex. कृपणेन समो दाता न भूतो न भविष्यति।
अस्पृशन्नेव वित्तानि यः परेभ्यः प्रयच्छति॥

—कवितामृतकूप, 129

This maxim is used to describe a miser, (a greedy person) who neither gives money to the needy nor uses it for his own pleasures. This miser does not use his wealth for others nor does he use it for his own benefit. Such wealth however, is generally stolen away by the thieves or lost in his presence. When a thing does not help the bearer, is practically lost before him. In this situation the man becomes helpless in spite of having plenty of wealth.

198. केकराक्षन्यायः

A squint eyed person looks at a point. But it appears that he is looking at some other point. This maxim is applicable to any such delusive appearance.

199. केतकीकुसुमन्यायः

भीमकान्तैर्नृपगुणैः स बभूवोपजीविनाम्।
अधृष्यश्चाभिगम्यश्च यादोरत्नेरिवार्णवः॥

–रघु. I.16.

The ketaki flower attracts everybody by its sweet fragrance. But men are afraid of plucking it, as they are afraid of the thorny sheath. The maxim states that the attractive things are difficult to be obtained because of some danger involved in approaching or obtaining them, as the people attracted by the precious jewels in the ocean take a deep dive but they are afraid of the dangerous. poisonous raptiles into it.

200. कैदारिकन्यायः

Cf. नीलकण्ठ 6.35

Kaidarika is a farmer. He provides irrigation facility to a particular part of the farm. After providing sufficient water to it, he closes it and turns the water to the unirrigated part. In shot, he manages to supply water to the entire farm. So also, says this maxim, the detachment starts from the mind and by continuous adherence to it, it spreads through out the body and then the Yogin witnesses a stream of detchment for his ultimate good.

201. कैमुतिकन्यायः

कैमुत्वेनार्थसंसिद्धिः काव्यार्थपत्तिरिष्यते।
स जितस्त्वन्मुखेनेन्दुः का वार्ता सरसीरुहाम्॥

'Kimuta' is used in the sense of 'What more needs to be said?' It is also used as follows:—how can the lesser persons dare do something which the eminent persons cannot do? This is also called Kāvyārthāpatti. This maxim can also be used to describe a situation when a particular meaning is not conveyed by individual means.

202. कोषपानन्यायः

In the days of yore, there were many ways of torturing a suspected criminal in which, making the culprit drink poison was one of the ways which is mentioned in this maxim.

203. कोष्ठपानन्यायः

This maxim tells about a drunkard who asserts that he drinks liquor in the house only. He does not drink anywhere outside. This stealthy method of developing vices is indicated by this maxim.

204. कौन्तेयराधेयन्यायः

Cf. राजपुत्र व्याद्दन्यायः, कर्णकौन्तेयन्यायः

Karṇa who was actually the son of Kunti, thought that

he was the son of Rādhā as he did not know about the secret of his birth. But when he came to know the truth about his birth, he really became the son of Kunti. On this the present maxim is based and it is applied to the fact that the concept that body is soul, vanishes and one come to know the reality by virtue of the advice of the teacher.

205. **क्रियाद्वयर्थकरी न्यायः**

मुमुक्षणा श्रोत्रियेण क्रियमाणं कर्म सत्त्वशुदिधद्वारा स्वस्य मोक्षहेतुर्भवति, वृष्टयादिद्वारा जगत्थितिहेतुश्च भवत्यत उभयथापि कर्म कर्तव्यमेवेति। —लौकिकन्याय, सा० 529

A good deed performed by a greatman shows two-fold result—

(i) He attains liberation by virtue of his pious act.

(ii) He helps sustaining the world.

206. **क्षतमक्षिकापातन्यायः**

Flies cling to the injured part of a person from which blood and flesh are exposed. Injured part itself is painful and when the flies cling to the exposed part, it becomes more painful and unbearable. This way of attacking a person on his weak points is the tendency of the wicked. This is what the maxim indicates.

—सा० 752

207. **क्षतेक्षारन्यायः**

If salt is sprinkled on a sore, the pain becomes unbearable. `This maxim suggests the cruel method of inflicting injuries on the already injured (mostly mentally).

208. **क्षीरदग्धजिह्वान्यायः**

दुध का जला छांछ भी फूककर पीता है। (Hindi)

Cf. दुधाने तोड भाजले की ताक सुद्दा फुकून पितात **(Marathi)**

If a man's tongue gets scalded by sipping boiled milk, he becomes fearfully cautious and drinks buttermilk also by blowing air into it to make it cool. A man becomes overcautious when he suffers from some painful happening.

209. क्षीरनिम्बन्यायः

The maxim tells that the original nature of a man cannot be changed by some artificial external device, as the bitterness of the Neem tree will not be diminished even if milk is poured to its roots instead of water.

210. क्षीरनीरन्यायः

Ex. हंसो हि क्षीरमादत्ते तन्मिश्रा आ वर्जयत्यपः॥

—अभिज्ञानशाकुन्तलम् VI.28

This milk water maxim says that when milk and water get mixed, they become inseparable. So when things and concepts are mixed or blended together inseparably, they indicate "Saṁkara". But when two things like dal and rice are mixed, they can be separated. This separable mixture is called "Saṁsṛṣṭi". They are together like the incarnation of Narasiṁha.

211. क्षीराब्धिवासिक्षीरकामनान्यायः

Viṣṇu once slept in the ocean of milk. There was no derth of milk for Him. But how unlucky it would be if he had to roam about in search of milk in the times of difficulty. Similarly, how unlucky will he be if a man has to move about in search of something which is found in abundance in his place?

212. खड्गकोशन्यायः

A sword is kept in a scabbard when it is not in use. If

a man runs away in fear, looking at an empty scabbard,he will be called the stupid coward. This maxim describes a man who feels frightened by some external appearance of danger.

213. खण्डितशाखान्यायः

The maxim states that even if a branch of a tree gives way, sprouts are seen growing from the place from which it is broken. Similarly, if a good or prosperous man loses something, it does not require much time for him to recover.

214. खपुष्पन्यायः

The flower of the sky is a fictitous notion. This maxim thereby, is applied to an impossible, non-existing thing!

215. खराश्वन्यायः

Cf. **खरीविषाणन्यायः**

This maxim hints at a wonderful and an astonishing situation and at the same time an impossible and an unimaginable thing in which a horse may be converted into an ass or vice versa.

216. खरीपाषाणन्यायः

'Kharī' means a vessel made of wood or stone. The maxim originates from a legend. A milk vender used to carry milk into two vessels, hanging on both the sides of the bamboo, and carrying the stick on his shoulders. Later he used to get one pot-full of milk only. So he tied a stone of equal weight on the other side of the stick. When the people asked him about the stone, he said if he carried only one vessel, he may lose the habit of carrying the weight of two pots. Moreover, the milk pot does not shake. All this shows that the milk vender had to face misfortune of carrying the weight of the stone also without any advantage. The maxim aims at this profitless act.

217. खरीविषाणन्यायः

The maxim aims at an impossible or an improbable matter like a female ass possessing horns.

218. खलेकपोतन्यायः

Ex. वृद्धा युवानः शिशवः कपोताः खले यथामी युगपत् पतन्ति।
तथैव सर्वे युगपत्पदार्थाः परस्परेणान्वयिनो भवन्ति॥

The maxim takes its origin from an incident. Pigeons see some grains on the ground of the field. All the pigeons alight on the field together and not individually or separately. Similarly, the words in a sentence convey the meaning of the sentence as a whole and not individually. This maxim also describes the events when many causes bring about one and the same effect. It is also the basis of the figure of speech called Samuccaya.

—सा० 183

219. खल्वाटबिल्वीयन्यायः

Ex. खल्वाटो दिवसेश्वरस्य किरणैः सन्तापितो मस्तके
वाञ्छन् देशमनातपं विधिवशात् तालस्य मूलं गतः।
तत्राप्यस्य महाफलेन पतता भग्नं सशब्दं शिरः
प्रायो गच्छति यत्र भाग्यरहितस्तत्रैव यान्त्यापदः॥

—भर्तृहरि नीतिशतकम्, 91

The maxim is based on one incident. A bald-headed person takes shelter under the shade of a Bilva tree, as he was tired after a long journey. But unfortunately, a ripe Bilva fruit falls on his head and his head breaks. This shows that an unlucky man faces trouble wherever he goes. His bad luck does not leave him. Detailed explanation of this maxim is given in a verse in Nītiśataka of Bhartṛhari.

220. गगनकुसुमन्यायः

Flower of the sky is an impossible, improbable thing, It is only an imaginative idea. It is quite impossible in reality. When some impossible thing is to be indicated, this maxim is used.

221. गगनारविंदन्यायः

This maxim tells about the lotus in the sky which is also an impossible, improbable thing. —सा० 715

222. गजघटान्यायः

Cf. **करिबृहितन्यायः**

The word 'Ghaṭā' means a herd or a group of elephants and hence the word 'Gaja' meaning elephant is not necessary. Such words are redundant. This maxim refers to such redundant usages.

223. गजानिमीलनन्यायः

Ex. देवीः कामयमानस्य चक्रे गजनिमीलिकाम्।

—राजतरंगिणी 6.721

When an elephant does not want to see something which is in front of it, it closes its eyes. According to this maxim, closing the eyes suggests indifference or feigning not to see anything.

224. गन्धर्वनगरन्यायः

The town of the Gandharvas is purely an imaginery, non-existent concept. This maxim is applicable to all such non-existent concepts.

225. गुडजिविह्विकान्यायः

If some bitter medicine is to be administered, some sweet thing like sugar or jaggery, is put on the tongue of the patient. The maxim based on this practice suggests that bitter things or thoughts can be made palatable by serving sweet things or thoughts.

226. गृहमार्जालन्यायः

The maxim says that the cat (domestic cat) moves happily in the house but the elephant has to roam outside. It is tied outside the house. Even then, the elephant gets more respect than the cat which is, living happily inside the house.

227. गोक्षीरन्यायः

If the buffalo milk is mixed with the cowmilk, there will not be any effect on cow milk. On the contrary, the entire milk becomes good and pious. Similarly good things are not affected by their contact with bad things.

228. गोक्षीरश्वदृतिन्यायः

If cow's milk which is considered to be very sacred and pious, is kept in a bag made of dog's skin, it will be certainly contaminated. So also, declares the maxim, that a man of spotless character might be affected, even to a certain extent, by keeping company with the man of bad character.

229. गोगवयन्यायः

A cow and a Gavaya (a wild buffalo) appear to be the same externally but the difference between the two can be noticed in their milk. The maxim tells us that the things which appear to be similar outwardly are not the same.

230. गोदोहनन्यायः

1. **काम्यसूक्तानां महाव्रते आज्यशस्त्रत्वेन यथोक्तानां गोदाहनन्यायेन पुरुषार्थत्वमेव, न क्रत्वर्थतम्।**

—जैमिनीयसूत्र, शाबरभाष्य, 4.1.2

2. **तस्माद्यथा क्रत्वाश्रयाण्यपि गोदोहनादीनि फलसंयोगादनित्यान्येवमुद्गीथाद्युपासनान्यपीति, द्रष्टव्यम्। अत एव कल्पसूत्रकारा नैवंजातीयकान्युपासनानि क्रतुषु कल्पयां- चक्रुः॥**

—ब्रह्मसूत्र, शाङ्करभाष्य, 3.3.42

The maxim refers to the act of milking a cow which is only an incidental event. Thus it indicates that somethings are related to some matters only casually and not essentially or generically.

231. गोपगृहिणीन्यायः

हत्वा नृपं पतिमवाप्य भुजङ्गदष्टं
देशान्तरे विधिवशाद् गणिकाऽस्मि जाता।
पुत्रं स्वकं समधिगम्य चितां प्रविष्टा
शोचामि गोपगृहिणी कथमद्य तक्रम्॥

This maxim is based on an anecdote—

Once a queen fell in love with some other person (a paramour). She gave birth to a child. Due to the excessive love for her lover, she killed the king by giving poison and ran to her paramour. When she came there, she was shocked to see her lover dead due to snake bite. Out of disappointment, she left the town and became a harlot in the adjoining place. One day, her own son, sufficiently grown up by that time, approached her. He recogized his mother and in a mood of penitence, threw himself in the burning fire. The harlot mother too threw herself into the river out of sorrow but was rescued by a cowherd boy whom she married later. But while selling the milk, she fell down and broke the pot. She had, thus, to face a series of calamities. The maxim points out the series of dangers which a man, lacking discretion, has to face.

—सा० 977

232. गोपुच्छन्यायः

The maxim refers to the tail of a cow which is quite thick at the beginning but gradually it becomes thinner and thinner. It is applied to the events which are conspicuous in the beginning but become insignificant later.

233. गोबलीवर्दन्यायः

Cf. ब्राह्मणवसिष्ठन्यायः

उक्षा भद्रो बलीवर्द ऋषभो वृषभो वृषः।
अनड्वान् सौरभेयो गौः. . . . .॥

बलीवर्दस्य गोविशेषत्वेऽपि बलीवर्दस्य झटिति गोत्वेन बोधनार्थं यथा प्रयोगस्तथान्ययोः सामान्यविशेषरूपयो र्झटिति बोधनार्थं प्रयोगस्तत्रास्य प्रवृत्तिः।

—भामती, पृ० 518, 537

"Bring the bovine animal and bring the bull"—The latter half of the sentence is not necessary. The order in the first part is sufficient, as Gau (in masculine gender) means bullock also. The combined use of 'Go' and Balivarda, however, particularly emphasizes that the bull should also be brought. The limitation of the meaning to 'bull' is done by the combined use of 'Go' and 'Balivarda'.

234. गोमयपायसन्यायः

यदि च चित्तेनैकेनानन्विताः स्वभावभिन्नाप्रत्यया जायेरन्नथ कथमन्यप्रत्ययदृष्टस्यान्यः स्मर्ता भवेत्।

अन्यप्रत्ययोपचितस्य च कर्माशयस्यान्यः प्रत्युपभोक्ता भवेत्। कथचित् समाधीयमानमध्ये तद् गोमयपायसीयन्यायमाक्षिपति।

—पातञ्जलयोगसूत्रभाष्य I.1.32

Though cowdung and milk are produced from the cow only, they cannot be taken to be the same, owing to their common origin. The same mind, for example, can give rise to multifarious thoughts.

235. गोमयवृश्चिकन्यायः

Ex. **दृश्यते हि लोके चेतनात्वेन प्रसिद्धवैभ्यः पुरुषादभ्यो विलक्षणानां केशनरवादीनामुत्पत्तिः, अचेतनत्वेन च प्रसिद्धेभ्यो गोमयादिभ्यो वृश्चिकादीनाम्।**

—ब्रह्मसूत्र, शाङ्करभाष्य, 2.1.6

The scorpions take their rise in the cowdung and thus they inherently exist in it. Similarly wicked nature of a wicked man is inherent in him. This inherent wickedness of the bad people is pointed out by this maxim. —सा० 890

236. गोमहिषीन्यायः

There is neither love nor enmity between the cows and the buffalos. They are two separate species. Similarly, there are some kings who are incapable of doing favour or showing frown (enmity) against anybody. This maxim aims at showing this extreme indifference of some persons.

237. गोमुखव्याघ्रन्यायः

Cf. **पयोमुखविषकुम्भन्यायः**

The maxim applies to a person who is cruel or pitiless like a tiger but puts on an innocent face outwardly like that of a cow.

238. गोवत्सन्यायः

If a cow is sold, it is taken for granted that the calf along with the cow is also sold. The maxim says that when a big transaction takes place, smaller transactions connected with it are supposed to have taken place.

239. गोविषाणन्यायः

अपार्थकमनायुष्यं गोविषाणस्य भक्षणम्।
दन्ताश्च परिधृष्यन्ते रसश्चापि न लभ्यते।

—महाभारत, शान्ति०, 128.57

The maxim aims at the stupidity of doing useless acts like eating of the horn of a cow which has no taste but it may result in breaking the teeth of the eater.

240. ग्रामदूरन्यायः

If one village is at a particular distance from another village, the distance from both the sides is the same. The maxim tells that there is no difference in the distance from one place to another and back again.

241. घटनिर्मातृभुवनविधातृकलहन्यायः

Ex. **हठादाकृष्टानां कतिपयपदानां रचयिता**
जनः स्पर्धालुश्चेदहह कविना वश्यवचसा।
भवेदद्य श्वो वा किमिह बहुना पापिनि कलौ
घटानां निर्मातुस्त्रिभुवनविधातुश्च कलहः॥

—भोजप्रबन्ध, 248; सा० 885

The man who manufactures a jar and the God who fashions the entire universe, are far different from each other. This maxim suggests that it is ridiculous for a man of inferior power to vie with a powerful, strong person.

242. घटप्रदीपन्यायः

Cf. **घटसूर्यबिम्बन्यायः**

If a lamp is placed inside a big jar, it illumines almost the entire part of the jar. Similarly, suggests the maxim that the man of knowledge (or wisdom) spreads his knowledge, though he may not remain in the light of publicity. This maxim can be explained thus. The influence of a person may have limited sphere as the lamp in the jar spreads light inside the entire part of the jar only.

243. घटारोहणन्यायः

This maxim indicates an ordeal in which the suspected criminal is asked to stand on a jar without trembling to prove his innocence.

244. घटाल्पदर्पणन्यायः

A jar, an elephant's temple and a mountain may be enormously big in their own way, but appear to be small when they are reflected in a mirror. This maxim steps in when bigger things are to be estimated with the help of small things.

245. घटियन्त्रन्यायः

आपद्गतं हससि किं द्रविणान्धमूढ
लक्ष्मीः स्थिरा न भवतीति किमत्र चित्रम्।
किं त्वं न पश्यसि घटीजलयन्त्रचक्रे
रिक्ता भवन्ति भरिता भरिताश्च रिक्ताः॥

—प्रबन्धचिन्तामणि, सा० 726

When the water-wheel rotates, the jars attached to it, go on moving up and down. The empty jars are filled with water from the well and those filled with water are emptied when they come up. This emptying and filling of the jars continue till the water-wheel rotates. This kind of situation is seen in man's life also. Happiness and sorrow, richness and poverty (emptiness) go on interchanging with each other. No state is permanent in the humanlife.

246. **घटीयन्त्रस्थितघटभ्रमान्यायः**

Ex. श्वासप्रश्वासयोर्गतिविच्छेदः प्राणायामः। स च वायुः सूर्योदयमारभ्य सार्धघटिकाद्वयं घटीयन्त्रस्थितघटभ्रमणन्यायेन एकैकस्यां नाड्यां भवति। एवं सत्यहर्निशं श्वासप्रश्वासयोः षट् छिताधिकैकविंशति-सहस्राणि जायन्ते।

This maxim is used when some events take place in a revolving fashion like the pitchers fixed in the water-wheel found in the fields.

247. **घट्टकुटीप्रभातन्यायः**

ननु स्फोटव्यञ्जकतापक्षोऽपि प्रागुक्ताविकल्पप्रसरेण घटकुटीप्रभातयितमिति चेत्, तदेतत् मनोराज्यादि जृम्भणम्।

This maxim is based on the event "Dawn at the toll gate". A driver drives his vehicle in a round about way, through lanes and bylanes in order to avoid the payment of toll amount. He goes on travelling like that in his vehicle and finally in the morning reaches a place which was nothing but the toll gate only. When a man tries consciously to avoid a particular thing unluckily, he has to face the same event, even after his conscious endeavour to avoid it. This maxim applies to such situations.

248. घरट्टन्यायः

The worldly life cannot be imagined with only one either a husband or a wife. Both are necessary for creation and for keeping the wheel of life moving. The maxim suggests this principle by giving the example of a grinding stone. Grinding takes place only with the help of two stones— one moving stone and the other a steady one.

249. घुणाक्षरन्यायः

—शिशुपालवध 3.68

Ex. श्रीर्निर्मिति प्राप्त घुणा क्षतैक वर्णोपमावाच्यमलं ममार्ज।
घुणोत्किरणात् कथंचिन्निष्पन्नमक्षरं घुणाक्षरम्।
तदिव यदकुशलेन दैवान्निष्पद्यते तद् घुणाक्षरीयम्।

When the white ants attack wood. those ants go on pricking inside the wood. With the dust particles coming out of these prickings, the shape of some lines or letters is formed incidentally. The maxim is used to describe certain events which take place very casually or accidentally.

250. घृतकोशातकीन्यायः

Ghṛta means ghee. Kośātaki is a type of gourd. The compound word means a gourd with ghee inside. But actually there is no ghee inside that fruit or vegetable. The word is a misnomer. The maxim describes such things (or persons,) the names of which are contradictory to their contents. The name of a person is Lakṣminārāyaṇa but he has no gold on his body.

251. घृतदग्धन्यायः

If water is sprinkled on burn injury, that will develop some sores on the burnt parts. Ghee is also a type of liquid. But when it is sprinkled on the wound, the burning sensation of the wound is not only reduced but no sores also come up. Ghee actually helps in healing the wound. So apparently, when things which appear malevolent, actually help the growth or healing. This is the purport of this maxim.

252. घोटकब्रह्मचारिन्यायः

A horse behaves like a detached passionless animal as long as it does not come across a mare (a female horse). But once it sees, it runs after the mare. Some people observe celibacy so long as they are away from the women. When they come across a damsel, they get lured by her. This restricted celibacy is the import of this maxim.

253. चक्रनाभिन्यायः

Cf. **अन्योन्याश्रयन्यायः।**

—महाभारत, शान्तिपर्व 118.1 Nīlakaṇṭha's commentary

The maxim hints at mutual dependence by giving an example of wheels of a cart which moves smoothly because of their being supported by the axis.

254. चक्रभ्रमणन्यायः

Ex. यथा दण्डापगमे संस्कारवशाच्चक्रं भ्रमति तथा विवेकिनापि देहधारणकर्मणोरक्षीणत्वान्न तत्क्षणान्मुक्तिः, किन्तूपभोगादिना कर्मक्षयादिति। तथा च श्रुतिः

दीक्षयैव नरो मुच्येत्तिष्ठेन्मुक्तोऽपि विग्रहे।
कुलालचक्रमध्यस्थो विच्छिन्नोऽपि भ्रमेद् घटः॥

न तावदनाश्रित्यारब्धकार्यं कर्माशयं ज्ञानोपत्तिरुपपद्यते। आश्रिते च तस्मिन् कुलालचक्रवत् प्रवृत्तवेगस्य प्रतिबन्धासम्भवाद् भवति वेगक्षयप्रतिपालनम्।

—ब्रह्मसूत्र, शाङ्करभाष्य, 4.1.15

A potter takes an earthen lump and places it on a rotating wheel to fashion a jar out of it. He makes use of a stick for making the wheel rotate swiftly. Though he withdraws the stick after some time, the momentum of the wheel continues. This maxim, based on this phenomenon, tells us that the original impressions or Saṁskaras persist though the external circumstances change.

255. चक्रवाकीचक्रवाकन्यायः

Ex. चक्रवाकवधुके आमन्त्रस्व सहचरम् उपस्थिता रजनी।

—अभिज्ञानशाकुंतलम् III; सा० 556

The maxim about the male and female Cakravāka birds, signifies the profound love between the lover and his beloved. These two birds move about happily together in the day time. But at the advent of the night both are separated. They move about through out the night in search of each other and cry piteously. These cakravāka birds are taken to be the ideal pair of lovers.

256. चक्षुर्दीपन्यायः

चक्षुर्दीपावपेक्ष्येते घटादेर्दशने यथा।
न दीपदर्शने किन्तु चक्षुरेकमपेक्ष्यते॥

—पञ्चदशी, 7.93

This maxim of eye and the lamp says that a jar is visible in the pitchy darkness depending on the contact of the eye with the jar. Even an eye alone does the work.Similarly,to remove the ignorance, about the

Brahman, only one, i.e. Vṛttivyāpti (the conscious feeling that I am the Brahman') is enough. The enlightenment does not expect any semblance of consciouseness (Cidābhāsa).

257. चक्षुःश्रवणन्यायः

The eyes of a serpent serve the purpose of the ears too. A serpent does the work of hearing and seeing simultaneously, with the same organ. This maxim is generally applicable to serpents only but it can be applied to a person who does the work of observing and listening at a time skilfully.

258. चण्डालकन्यकान्यायः

A king who had married a cāṇḍala lady, was riding on an elephant along with his spouse. The king got down from the elephant only to greet a sage respectfully. The cāḍala lady thought that the sage is highly respectable and began to walk with him. The sage, on the way, stopped to pay obeissance to lord Śiva. The lady, then, sat in the temple only. After some time, a dog came there and eased itself on the shrine of Śiva. When the dog began to loiter around the cāṇḍala lady, she thought that the caṇḍala is superior to all. The maxim suggests that the people come back to their original nature, even after taking efforts for sustaining superior positions.

259. चतुर्वेदविन्न्यायः

This maxim refers to an anecdote. It is a custom to offer some charity to a person who knows (i.e. has mastered) the four vedas. A person approached a wealthy man and solicited charity from him, pleading that he knows that the number of vedas is four. This was clearly an act of cheating. Similarly, if a person knows and mutters some words, related to the Brahman, cannot be taken to be the knower of the Brahman.

260. चतुर्व्यूहन्यायः

In many sects four deities are mentioned who are connected with worldly, spiritual and divine manner with the universe.

261. चन्दनगुणन्यायः

किं तेन हेमगिरिणा रजताद्रिणा वा यत्राश्रिताश्च मन्यामहे मलयमेव यदाश्रयेण कङ्कोलनिम्बकुटजा अपि चन्दनाः स्युः॥

—भर्तृहरिवैराग्य 2.78

The sandal tree grows in plenty in some areas of the Malaya mountain. It offers its fragrance to other trees which grow in that area. The maxim based on this phenomena, says that even the wicked men derive some goodness by remaining in the company of good and virtuous people.

262. चन्द्रचन्द्रिकान्यायः

अतः सर्वदेवकारणस्य रुद्रस्य या शक्तिश्चन्द्रचन्द्रिकान्यायेन, तदुद्बोधरूपिणी स्वाधीनवल्लभेति प्रसिद्धा सैव भवानी।

—आनन्दगिरि

The maxim based on many inseparable things which are as inseparable as the moon and the moonlight.

263. चन्दनन्यायः

शरीरैकदेशसम्बद्धोऽपि सन् सकलदेहव्यापिनमाह्लादं करोति इत्येवमात्माऽपि देहैकदेशस्थः सकलदेहव्यापिनीमुपलब्धिं करिष्यति। —ब्रह्मसूत्र, शाङ्करभाष्य, 2.3.23-24

This maxim states that the sandal paste applied to on

part of the body, renders the entire body fragrant. Similarly, the self(soul residing in one part of the body) (i-e. heart) with its existence is felt in the entire body.

264. चन्द्रचकोरन्यायः

The bird called cakora eagerly waits for the rising of the moon, as it drinks the rays of the moon only. It does not eat anything except the rays of the moon.If some body waits for some particular person anxiously, this maxim is used.

265. चन्द्रज्योत्स्नान्यायः

Cf. करिबृहितन्यायः, गजघटाव्यायः

चन्द्रज्योत्स्नाशरदि पुलिने सैकतेऽस्मिन् सरषा
वादद्यूतं चिरतरमभूत् सिद्धयूनोः कयोश्चित्।
एको वक्ति प्रथमनिहतं कैटभं कंसमन्यः
स त्वं तत्त्वं कथय भगवन् को हतस्तत्र पूर्वम्॥

Joytsnā means moonlight only. There is no need of using a prefix 'moon' to it . The maxim is used when such redundancy is to be conveyed.

—सा० 210

266. चन्द्रातपमलन्यायः

सितेतर इव त्येषः पक्षश्चित्रं न कर्षति।
चन्द्रातपमलन्यायः प्रवासमलिनीकृतः॥

Looking at the moon and especially its black spot, somebody points out that the moon has become black due to tiresome journey in the sky. The moon has offered the moonlight to the entire world and so she has become pale and dark. The blackish, dark moon does not appear pleasing. According to this maxim, even a beautiful object may not be considered appealing and beautiful all the time.

267. चम्पकपटन्यायः

If fragrant flowers are wrapped in a piece of cloth, the cloth gives out fragrance for some time, owing to its contact with the sweet, fragrant flowers; though the flowers are taken away. Similarly, says the maxim that one can imbibe certain good qualities in the company of the great people.

268. चविर्तचर्वणन्यायः

The maxim refers to the rumination of something which is already ruminated. Thus it suggests the repetition of the same thing again and again.

269. चातकजीमूतन्यायः

It is the nature of the Cātaka bird to drink that water only which falls from the clouds i-e.rain water. Even though there is plenty of water on the earth, this bird does not dare to look at it. It quenches its thirst by the rainwater only. It is its nature. The maxim describes the nature of certain persons as quite natural, though it may appear to be queer.

270. चालनीन्यायः

When a sieve is used, it drops the flour down and retains the chaff into the sieve. Taking clue from the fact that the sieve accepts the chaff and drops out the good grains or flour. The maxim describes the mentality of some persons of this type.

271. चित्रतुरगन्यायः

When the actor acts on the stage, the ancilliaries Vibhāvas, etc, are artificial and not real. The spectators then, infer some permanent moods. (स्थायीभाव) and then enjoy some particular scenes. This is compared with a picture of the horse on which the maxim is based. The painted horse gives the idea of a real horse on the basis of the imagined ancilliaries. Real events are inferred by the spectators.

272. चित्रपटन्यायः

Before drawing a picture, the artist spreads some white paint on the canvas. Then he draws some lines on it and then applies various colours to the picture. Similarly, the God appears to be consciousness or God. Then He becomes an indweller and finally bears a virāṭ figure.

—सा० 285

273. चित्राङ्गनान्यायः

Cf. चित्रानलन्यायः, चित्रामृतन्यायः

A lady is directly seen in a picture but she in not capable of giving the pleasure of kissing or embracing. Similarly, the nectar pot or the fire, painted in a picture, are unable to show their effects. The present maxim, based on these examples, suggests that the actions performed by an enlightened person does not show any result. Thus the actions performed by an enlightened person do not cling to him.

274. चित्रिताङ्गजम्बुकन्यायः

It will be ridiculous if a jackal tries to imitate a panther or a tiger. The jackal tries to adore its body with various colours and thus tries to imitate a tiger. The maxim thus ridicules the attempt of low persons who try to imitate the greatmen externally.

275. चौरापराधान्माण्डव्यनिग्रहन्यायः

भेदवादिनं प्रति इमानि दूषणान्युद्घुष्यन्ते किं वा धर्मिभेदवादिनं प्रति। प्रथमे चौरापराधान्माण्डव्यनिग्रहन्यायापातः।

—सर्वदर्शनसङ्ग्रह, पृ० 73; सा० 123

This maxim alludes to a legend. Once some thieves stole some precious articles from the royal palace. The police began to chase them. Being afraid of the royal police, they threw away those things near the sage Māṇḍavya who was silently practising penance. The police thought that the sage had stolen the things and produced the sage before the king who sentenced him to death. This maxim tells that even good and innocent persons suffer, owing to the cruel deeds of the wicked.

276. छत्रिन्यायः

Ex. एकस्तत्र कर्मफलं पिबति, भुङ्क्ते नेतरस्थापि। पातृसम्बन्धात् पिबन्तावित्युच्यते छत्रिन्यायेन।

—कठोपनिषद्, शाङ्करभाष्य, 3.1

When it is said that the umbrella men are passing by, it is also implied that there are many men without umbrella also who are passing out with them. The maxim suggests that any objective expression is based on the prominent principal aspect.

277. छागपशुन्यायः

This maxim refers to the semantic law of contraction where meanings of some words are contracted in certain contexts. In Sanskrit ('Paśu') animal means all animal including an ox but in Vedic language, the meaning of this word animal (Paśu) is contracted. It means only goat, especially one which is offered in a sacrifice.

278. छायापिशाचन्यायः

आत्माज्ञानमलं निरस्तममलं प्राप्तं च तत्त्वं परं
कण्ठस्थाभरणादिवद् भ्रमवशाच्छायापिशाची यथा।

(—From the commentary of Nṛsimha Sarasvatī on Vedāntasāra

Sometimes a person sees some shadow and thinks it to be a goblin. This maxim describes some such delusion.

279. छुरिकाकूष्माण्डन्यायः

तेजसां हि न वयः समीक्ष्यते।

–रघुवंश XI. 1.

If a small knife can cut a big pumpkin, a small, healthy boy can subdue a weak grown up person. This is the import of this maxim.

280. जतुकाष्ठन्यायः

In Sanskrit, there are two types of pun—Sabhanga and Abhanga. In Sabhanga type, one word is closely connected with the other word (but in different sense). That is when the two are glued together like lac and wood, they illustrate the Sabhanga panaromasia.

281. जपास्फटिकन्यायः

Ex. यथा स्फटिके जपाकुसुमाश्रिते लौहित्यं विवेकिनां प्रतीत एवास्ति, न वस्तुतः।
एवमात्मानि ईश्वराधीने विवेकिनां कर्तृत्वं प्रतीत एवास्ति, न वस्तुतः इति वक्तुं शक्यम्।

–मधुसूदन सरस्वती, गीताभाष्य 18.9

If a chinarose flower is kept near a crystal, the crystal appears to have assumed red hue, though actually it does not become red. This maxim indicates this type of delusion.

282. जम्बुकारग्वधन्यायः

Once a fox ate a fruit of the tree "Casula fistula". Owing to that its stomach started aching. Then it decided not to touch that fruit again. But as soon as the stomach-ache reduced, the jackal went in search of that fruit and ate it again. This maxim illustrates the uncontrolled longing of a greedy person.

283. जलकतकरेणुन्यायः

A 'Kataka' fruit, when put in muddy water, makes the water clear and is ultimately dissolved in it. This maxim based on this example, suggests that the knowledge sublates that which deserves sublation and then it disappears. —सा० 260

284. जलचन्द्रन्यायः

Ex. एक एव तु भूतात्मा भूतेभूते व्यवस्थितः।
एकदा बहुधा चैव दृश्यते जलचन्द्रवत्॥

The reflections of the moon in various pots, filled with water are different but the moon is one only. Similarly, says the maxim, the self appears to be multi- numbered in many bodies in many shapes but is actually one only.

285. जलतरङ्गन्यायः

Ex. माधुर्यद्रव शैत्यादिनीरधर्मास्तरङ्गके।
अनुपन्थाय तभिष्ठे फेनेऽप्यनुभिगता यथा।

—सा० 638

When breezes blow over the surface of water, many billows are formed, together with foam and the like. Though they appear to be different, they contain the properties of water. Thus the maxim says, there may appear different shapes of effects, though the cause is one only.

286. जलतरङ्गबुद्बुदन्यायः

Ex. चेतनाचेतनप्रणञ्चस्य जले तरङ्गबुद्बुदन्यायेन तत्रैवोत्पत्ति-प्रलययोः श्रवणादेव योनिः सर्वस्य प्रभवाप्ययौ हि भूतानामिति तदन्यत्वात् सर्वस्येति भाव इत्युक्तम्।

–महाभारत, सभापर्व, 40, 14 (Nīlakaṇṭha's commentary)

Billows and bubbles originate in water, remain in the water for some time and then dissolve in the water, which is their place of origin and they are not at all different from water.

287. जलतुम्बिका न्यायः

Jalatumbikā is a pumpkin like fruit which floats on the water so long as the mud applied to it remains intact. But it sinks in the water when the mud is washed away. Similarly, says the maxim, that a man can sustain himself as long as he has some supporting base. When it disappears he sinks.

288. जलतैलन्यायः

When oil is poured on the boiling water, the boiling water becomes cool and calm. Similarly, the wrath of an angry man can be removed by sweet, affectionate words. This is the spirit of this maxim.

289. जलतैलबिन्दुन्यायः

If a drop of oil is poured on the water, it spreads all over the water, but a drop of ghee gets solidified in the same place. This expansion and contraction of the two substances points out the two different natures of men also by this maxim.

390. जलबिन्दुनिपातन्यायः

जलबिन्दुनिपातेन क्रमशः पूर्यते घटः।
स हेतुः सर्वविद्यानां धर्मस्यच धनस्य च॥

—चाणक्यनीति 12.19

If the water falls down drop by drop from some place, it may fill a big pitcher also. Even though the drop of water is very small, if it falls continuously, it is possible to fill up a big jar with that water. Similarly, the great tasks show a small beginning but these small things may lead to the magnificent ends—says the maxim.

291. जलमन्थनन्यायः

The maxim decries the futile attempt of churning the water. If milk or curd is churned, we get butter but if water is churned, a person does not get anything. It will result in fruitless, tiresome effort. This maxim applies to such useless, futile efforts of the person.

292. जलमौक्तिकन्यायः

Ex. (1) महाभारत, अनुशासन० 12.9 नीलकण्ठ टीका
(2) भर्तृहरि, नीतिशतक, 33.

(सन्तप्तायसि..............स्वात्त्यां सागरशुक्तिसम्पुटगतं तज्जायते मौक्तिकम्।)

An ordinary man can become great if there are favourable circumstances. The maxim underscores this truth by showing the example of a pearl, if it falls in a sea-shell in the days, marked by Svāti star it is converted into a pearal.

293. जलाक्षरन्यायः

It will be futile for a person to draw some lines on the

water. The water. unlike a paper or a canvas is not suitable for writing. The maxim suggests that proper basis or substratum is necessary for doing anything.

294. जलाग्निन्यायः

The fire and the water are two contradictory things in nature. They cannot stay together. When they come together forcibly, the stronger one wins and the weaker one has to perish. Similarly, two enemies cannot stay together for a long time. The destruction of one of them is certain. The inferior or the weaker has to face a defeat and ultimately he has to die.

295. जलानयनन्यायः

When one work is to be done, it is taken for granted that the ancillaries are taken care of. For example, when somebody is asked to bring water, he is not reminded of fetching the water in a glass or a jug.

296. जलालोकपवनन्यायः

The maxim informs that the water, the air and the firmament are never mutually antagonistic.

297. जलाशयतरङ्गचन्द्रन्यायः

This maxim tells about optical illusion. The reflection of the moon is only one in the still water. But numerous reflections are visible in the moving or waving water due to optical illusion.

298. जघ्नौकान्यायः

If a leech is placed on the massive breasts of a damsel, it will suck only blood of the breast, instead of the sweet milk in it. Similarly, the wicked person, always looks at the bad things in a person without appreciating his good qualities. They are the fault finders and do not care to look at the virtues of any person says the maxim.

299. जलौष्ण्यन्यायः

Ex. उष्णत्वमग्न्यातपसम्प्रयोगाच्छैत्यं हि यत्साप्रकृतिजलस्य

–रघुवंश 5. 54

The water is basically cool only. It becomes hot when heat is applied to it. There is one natural quality in any object and the other quality is either adopted, derived or a temporary attribute. This is the meaning of this maxim.

300. जहत्स्वार्थवृत्तिन्यायः

Sometimes the words give up their expressed meaning (Abhidhārtha). Just as a man working for somebody else, gives up his own work. Similar event takes place in semantic parlance and some secondary meaning becomes prominent. The event is called Jahallakṣaṇā, in which the function of the word gives up its direct meaning. This is the intent of the maxim.

301. जहदजहत्स्वार्थवृत्तिन्यायः

When the meaning is partially given up and is retained partially, it becomes the case of Jahadjahatsvārtha Vṛttinyāya.

302. जातेष्टिन्यायः

Cf. याज्ञवल्क्यस्मृति, मिताक्षरा 5.220.

'Jātakarma' rite is performed as soon as the child is born. This is the first ceremony of the child after his birth. Offerings are given in a sacrifice which is performed at the time of a child's birth. But the question is—Who is the beneficiary of the oblations offered? the answer is the newly born child.

303. जामातृशुद्धिन्यायः

पण्डितोपदिष्टं सर्वथा मौनमेवालम्बमानो (महिषीपालः) राजकन्यकया तद्वैदग्ध्यजिज्ञासया नवलिखितपुस्तकस्य। शोधनाय उपरुद्धः। ....प्रसिद्धिभूत्॥

—प्रबन्धचिन्तामणि

The maxim refers to the act of trying to give a book for reading to the son-in-law which is tantamount to ask an ignorant dull man to do some intellectual work.

304. जामात्रर्थं प्रस्तुतस्य सूपादेरतिथ्युपकारकत्वमितिन्यायः

The maxim suggests that even if the food is prepared mainly for the son-in-law, it can be served for the other guests also.

Some arguments are advanced in the Brahmasūtra to refute the doctrine of the Sāṁkhyas that the cause of the world is Pradhāna. According to this maxim, the arguments can be utilized for refuting the same Pradhāna doctrine of the Yogic theorists.

305. जालमत्स्यन्यायः

This maxim tells that a fish caught in a net can see things outside but it cannot come out from the net. Similarly, a person caught in the snare of worldly passions or delusions may understand the evil effects of his position but cannot come out of it.

306. टिट्टिभन्यायः

This maxim refers to an anecdote. The ocean used to destroy the eggs of a female osprey. The male bird lodged a complaint with Garuḍa who reported the matter to Viṣṇu. At the behest of Viṣṇu, Garuḍa began to dry up the ocean by flapping his huge wings.

The ocean felt frightened and returned the eggs to the osprey. The moral of this story and maxim is that God helps those who are diligent and are devotees of Him. Secondly a man can do wonders if he is of firm mind and takes firm decisions.

307. डमरुकमणिन्यायः

अन्यार्थमिति मध्यवर्तिपदं डमरुकमणिन्यायेनोभयत्रापि सम्बद्धनीयम्। (From the commentary of Mallisena on Syādvādmañjari).

A string is tied to the Damaru (tabor like small musical instrument). There is a small wooden piece, tied to the string, at the centre. When a person plays that instrument, he tosses the Damaru, so that the wooden piece at the centre strikes on both the leather-covered sides of it and makes sound. This maxim describes the helping nature of a neutral middleman.

308. तक्रकौण्डिण्यन्यायः

Cf. याज्ञवल्क्यस्मृति 3.257.

Ex. नहि भवति ब्राह्मणोभ्यो दधि दीयतां तक्रं कौण्डिय-न्यायवेति विकल्पस्तस्माद द्वयोरपि सामान्य विषयत्वमेव।

लोके हि सत्यपि सम्भवे बाधनं भवति। तद्यथा दधि ब्राह्मणेभ्यो दीयतां तक्रं कौण्डिन्याय, इति सत्यपि सम्भवे दधिदानस्य तक्रदानं निवर्तकं भवति।

—पतञ्जलि महाभाष्य पाणिनि, 1.1.47

An event is narrated to explain this maxim.

When direction is given to serve curds to all the Brāhmaṇas, and buttermilk to Kauṇḍiṇya, though Kauṇḍiṇya was entitled to get curds, as he was also a Brahmaṇa, this was an exception. The maxim shows that a general rulẹ is set aside by a specific rule. This shows that there are exceptions to the general rule also.

309. तटाकपरीवाहन्यायः

Cf. पूरोत्पीडे तडागस्य परीवारः प्रतिक्रिया॥

—उत्तररामचरित III.29

When the lake starts overflowing, the boundary bunds or walls would be endangered. So the additional water of the lake is allowed to escape through some artificial fissures. So also when somebody's heart is overwhelmed with grief, efforts are made to make that person weep, so that the pressure of grief would be reduced.

310. तण्डुलभक्षणन्यायः

When rice is properly prepared, one can eat it with pleasure. But if it is not well-cooked, one has to eat the half-cooked rice only. The maxim suggests that one has to deal with the situation as it is.

311. तत्प्रख्यन्यायः

तत्प्रख्यं चान्यशास्त्रम्। तस्य गुणस्य प्रख्यं प्रापकमन्यशास्त्रं यत्र भवति।

—सा० 853

When an injunction is given that oblations should be given to the fire (which is tended), the question, as to what oblations should be given, arises. The answer is that oblations should be given, based on the strength of the word Agnihotra.

312. तन्तुन्यायः

When many threads are brought together, they are

able to weave a cloth. Similarly, suggests the maxim that the great men should come together to accomplish a noble task. —सा० 994

313. तप्ततैलाम्बुन्यायः

This maxim refers to an ordeal in which hot water or hot oil was poured on the body of the suspected criminal. This was also one of the ordeals, a crimal had to face, to prove his innocence or guiltlessness.

314. तप्तपरशुग्रहणन्यायः

Ex. स यदि तस्य कर्ता भवति, तत एवानृतमात्मानं कुरुते, सोऽनृताभिसन्धोऽनृतेनात्मानमन्तर्धाय परशु तप्तं प्रतिगृह्णाति, स दह्यतेऽथ हन्यते।

—छान्दोग्योपनिषद् 6.16

In the days of yore, many ordeals were employed to test the criminals. Sometimes, suspected criminal was asked to hold a heated axe. If it burns his hand, his crime was confirmed or otherwise he was declared guiltless.

315. तप्तभ्राष्टतिलन्यायः

Cf. पातञ्जलमहाभाष्य I.1.50.

If seasemum seeds are placed on a hot pan, they will be burnt down immediately. Their original condition will not remain for a moment and they will be burnt down completely. This maxim is used in the Mahābhāṣya.

316. तप्तमाक्षिकोद्धरणन्यायः

The maxim also refers to a type of ordeal, in which hot wax is to be taken out with the hand by the suspected criminal.

317. तप्तायःपिण्डन्यायः

Ex. इदमेव तुरीयं शुद्धचैतन्यमज्ञानादि तदुपहितचैतन्याभ्यां तप्तायः पिण्डवद विविकतम्।

—वेदान्तसार, पृ० 51

If an iron ball is heated, no smoke comes out of it but it will become red, hot and burn the hand. It has all the effects of fire in it without smoke.

318. तप्तायसपत्रबिन्दुन्यायः

This maxim maintains that the virtues of a good person disappear if he comes in contact with the wicked, as water, poured on a hot iron evaporates completely.

319. तमःप्रकाशन्यायः

The maxim refers to those persons who are mutually enmical and try to remove one another as darkness and light are mutually enmical to each other.

320. तमोदीपन्यायः

Ex. अज्ञानं ज्ञातुमिच्छेद्यो मानेनात्यन्तमूढधीः।
स तु नूनं तमः पश्येद्दीपेनोत्तमतेजसा॥

—वेदान्तसिद्धान्तमुक्तावलि

The maxim emphasizes the fact that the knowledge obliterates the ignorance, as a lamp removes the darkness.

321. तरक्षडाकिनीन्यायः

पायसान्नाप्रिया त्वक्स्था पशुलोकभयङ्करी।
अमृतादिमहाशक्तिसंवृता डाकिनीश्वरी॥

—ललितासहस्त्रनाम, 99

This maxim refers to the merciless nature of some

men who are bent on tormenting others, like Ḍākiṇī, a form of the Goddess, sitting on a tiger and deploying her cruel disposition.

322. तस्करकन्दन्यायः

**Ex. अशक्ये विनियुक्तोऽपि कृष्णलाग् श्रपयेदिति।
सर्वात्मनाऽप्यसौ कुर्वन् कुर्यातस्करकन्दुवत्॥**

—सुरेश्वराचार्य

This maxim is based on a legend. Once a thief was caught in a kitchen. The thief pleaded that he was a cook, and that he was appointed as a cook in some house. But once he was caught red handed, stealing some articles in the kitchen. This shows that the tendency to do some thing beyond ones scope or capacity ultimately ruins a person.

323. तालवृक्षच्छायान्यायः

A palmyra tree grows tall but it can never give good shadow to the travellers. The fruits of this tree also grow on such a height that the passers by cannot pluck and eat them. Similarly, a person may be occupying a high position like the tall, great palmyra tree. But he is of no use for his fellowmen who seek shelter or help from him. What is the use of his greatness? The maxim describes people, who are great but useless for the society.

324. तालसर्पन्यायः

If a serpent wants to eat a fruit of the palmyra tree, it cannot do so because the knots of the tree are bent upwards and as such it cannot climb. Moreover, the belly of the serpent is likely to be torn while climbing it. This maxim thus advises that one should not go to a place, fraught with danger, to obtain some fruit.

325. तिलतण्डुलन्यायः

लिम्पतीव तमोऽङ्गानि वर्षतीवाञ्जनं नभः।
असत्पुरुषसेनेव दृष्टिर्विफलतां गता॥

—मृच्छकटिक I.14

Sesamum seeds and rice grains can be separated, even if they are mixed i.e. they maintain their separate identity. They do not mix like milk and water and become one. In the figure of speech, if more than one figures of speech are found in a line or in a verse, such a blending of the figure of speech is called "Samsṛṣṭi"

326. तीरबकन्यायः

This maxim describes a person who pretends to be calm and uninvolved but acts swiftly when some personal benefit or self-interest is involved; exactly like a crane who stands quietly closing eyes on the bank of a river, pretending that it is practising meditation, but when a fish comes within its range, it catches and swallows it swiftly.

327. तीर्थकाकन्यायः

Generally, when people visit the places of pilgrimage, they take bath in the sacred water of the river there. A crow, however, takes dip in the same sacred river many a time without knowing that the dip is meritorious. This maxim suggests that some people are not equipped or qualified for deriving merit even at the sacred places.

328. तुम्बीविकलन्यायः

A man requires some ancillaries to do some work efficiently. To illustrate this, the maxim says that a lute will not produce melifluous sounds unless it has a pumpkin like wooden device.

329. **तुलायष्टिन्यायः (तुलादण्डयष्टिन्याय)**

स्तोकेनोन्नतिमायाति स्तोकेनायात्यधो गतिम्।
अहो सुसदृशी चेष्टा तुलाकोटेः खलस्य च॥

—हितोपदेश 1.154

When the things are kept in a pan of the balance, they affect the balance and the balancing rod begins to tilt. So is the state of a wicked man who keeps on changing according to the surroundings—says the maxim.

330. **तुलोन्नमनन्यायः**

If one pan of the balance is raised up, the other one goes down. This maxim is applied to the work which puts forth simultaneous results. A man thinks that, if one of the rivals is subdued, it will be easy for him to subdue others.

331. **तुल्यबलप्रेसणन्यायः**

If two associates are of equal strength, one will try to use the other for his own benefit. But if they are sent on errand at different places, and if their work subserves the same purpose, both of them cannot accomplish the work at the same time.

332. **तुषकण्डन्यायः**

Ex. Cf. पिष्टपेषणन्याय

अविचारवतो युक्तिकथनं तुषकण्डनम्।
नीचेषूपकृतं राजन् वालुकास्विव मूत्रितम्॥

—हितोपदेश 4.13

Pounding the chaff of the corn does not serve any purpose. The maxim tells that it is fruitless to waste one's energy on useless tasks.

—सा० 409

333. तुष्यतुदुर्जनन्यायः

If in a dispute, one accepts the view of the disputant only temporarily, this maxim which means,'Let the wicked fellow be satisfied', comes into picture.

334. तृणजलौकान्यायः

This maxim tells about a caterpillar which moves from one blade of grass to the other one slowly and cautiously. It does not leave the earlier blade without securing the other one. This describes a cautious, careful nature of a person. It also refers to an individual self which abandons earlier body only when the next embodiment is secured.

335. तृणभक्षणन्यायः

In the olden days, a person used to carry blade of grass between his teeth which indicated his intention of surrendering. Here eating should be taken to mean "holding". A person's self-respect also is hurt in this act of surrendering by holding a blade of grass with his teeth.

336. तृणरज्जुन्यायः

(i) बहूनामल्यसाराणां समवायो दुरत्ययः।

—भोजप्रबन्ध 145

(ii) तृणैरावेष्ट्यते रज्जुर्यया नागोऽपि बध्यते।

—सुभाषित

This maxim tells about the strength of unity. A blade of grass is very weak but if a number of blades are tied together, the rope so formed, controls even the mighty intoxicated elephant.

337. तृणारणिमणिन्यायः

Ex. (i) न तु वह्निच्छिन्नं प्रति तृणादेः कारणत्वम्, परस्पर-व्यभिचारात्, एवं यत्र कार्यकारणभाव बाहुल्यं कार्यतावच्छेदकं कारणभावच्छेदकं च नाना तत्रास्य प्रवृत्तिः।

—लौकिक साहस्त्री, पृ० 145

(ii) (शक्ति निर्पुणताभ्यासाः) समुदिता दण्डचक्रादि न्यायेन परस्परसापेक्षाः व्यस्ताः तृणारमणिन्यायेन प्रत्येकं कार्यजनकः

—काव्यप्रकाश, इळकीकरटीका, पृ० 13

This maxim is related to the fact that different causes produce one type of effect. The grass, the. Araṇi pieces of wood and the jewel give rise to fire but the causes of producing fire are different viz. blowing, rubbing and falling of the rays of the sun respectively.

—सा० 433

338. दग्धपटन्यायः

विज्ञप्तिमात्र देहास्ते न तेषां जन्मकर्मणी।

—योगवासिष्ठ, निर्वाण उत्तरार्ध 142.24

जन्मग्रहणं दग्धपटन्यायेन देहस्थितिप्रदर्शनार्थम्।

—सा० 593

(i) This maxim tells that even if something is lost, feelings or pride about the lost aricles remain intact, as the marks on a cloth do not disappear, even though it is burnt

(ii) The shape of a piece of cloth, though burnt down, remains intact. So also, even though the wealth is lost, the pride about it, is never lost.

339. दग्धपत्रन्यायः

Cf. दग्धरशनान्यायः

This maxim comes into force when a leaf is burnt. Its shape remains almost intact. One can get some idea about an object even though it is burnt down. Similarly, the original nature of a man does not change, even though he faces many ups and downs in his life.

340. दग्धपदमार्जालन्यायः

This maxim is based on a funny story where the loss is supposed to have been reverted to the complainer. Four persons, engaged in the business of cotton, had domesticated a cat. They tried to fasten small bells to its foot, when it was injured. They bandaged the leg but it caught fire. The cat ran with the burning bandage towards the heap of cotton and the entire cotton bales were burnt. When the merchants sought justice, the judge declared that the cat cannot walk towards the heap of cotton and so the three other merchants who were not involved in tying the bells, should pay the compensation.

341. दग्धबीजन्यायः

The maxim maintains that when the ignorance is removed, the mundane world also is annulled, as the burnt seeds do not germinate.

342. दग्धरशनान्यायः

Cf. दग्धपत्रन्यायः

When a three-plied rope is burnt, the shape of the three plies remains as it is. The appearance is false, as the rope is completely burnt down. So also maintains the maxim that for a man of enlightenment, the world is unreal though it may appear to be real.

—सा० 283

343. दग्धेन्धनवह्निन्यायः

Ex. दग्धदहन न्यायेन यावद्प्राप्तं विधीयते।

—काव्यप्रकाश V.

The fire which burns fuel, extinguishes automatically in the absence of fuel, and abandons its special state of flame. So also, when the mental functions are curbed,the inner apparatus is calmed down in pure Sattva state. The maxim tells that with the disappearance of Vṛttis or mental functions, only the Sattva quality survives.

344. दण्डसर्पमारणन्यायः

When a person sees a serpent, he tries to find a stick to strike at it. But instead of the stick, he comes across an axe and his efforts to find out a stick go waste. This maxim describes a situation when a thing which could have been obtained without any effort, is obtained with effort. —सा० 251

345. दण्डापूपन्यायः

(i) **मूषिकेण दण्डो भक्षित इत्यनेन तत्सहचरितमपूप भक्षणमर्थादायातं भवतीति नियतसमानन्यायाद र्थान्तरमापतनीत्येव न्यायो दण्डापूपिकः।**

(iii) याज्ञवल्क्यस्मृति मिताक्षराटीका–2.126
सम्भावितस्यस्वातन्त्रस्य पितृस्थानीयस्य ज्येष्ठस्यापि दोषं वदता ज्येष्ठपरतन्त्राणां कनीयसां पुत्रस्थानीयानां दण्डापूपनीत्या सुतरां दोषो दर्शित एव।

Once some cakes were affixed to a stick. A person brought the news that the stick was eaten by a mouse. The eating up of a stick conveys that the cakes have also been eaten. the maxim based on this incident shows that when something is destroyed, things associated with it are also supposed to have been destroyed.

346. दण्डिन्यायः

Cf. छत्रिन्यायः

Some persons, walking on the street, carry sticks in their hand and some of them do not have sticks with them. Still the group is termed as "the one carrying stick"

347. दधिक्षीरन्यायः

Milk is transformed into curds. This change is "transformation". But the change of rope into a serpent is false and so it is called false change (i.e. Vivarta). The Advaita Vedāntins believe that the worldly phenomenon is a false change (i.e. Vivarta).

348. दम्पतीकलहन्यायः

This maxim describes the natural love between the husband and the wife. Sometimes it appears that there is no love lost between them, especially when they quarrel bitterly but ultimately both of them display their mutual love.

349. दर्पणप्रतिबिम्बन्यायः

Ex. अन्तरस्मिन्निमे लोका अन्तर्विश्वमिदं जगत्।
बहिर्वन्मायया भाति दर्पणे प्रतिबिम्बवत्॥

The worldly phenomenon of the world is reflected in the Brahman, as objects are reflected in the mirror.

350. दर्पणमुखावलोकनन्यायः

The mirror gives the exact and correct reflection of a thing. If the thing is ugly or dirty, the reflection will be ugly but if it is beautiful, it will give beautiful reflection. This is the meaning of this maxim.

351. दर्वीपाकरसन्यायः

A spoon is placed in a vessel, containing some soup for taking it out and serving. The spoon is in contact with the soup or curry for a long time; but it cannot relish the taste of the soup. So also, an ignorant man cannot learn or know anything, even though he is surrounded by books or learned men.

352. दशमविवेकन्यायः

This maxim is based on a legend. Ten stupid fellows went on a journey. At one place, one of them began to count his co-travellers. He counted them (barring himself) and complained that somebody was missing. Another person started counting in the same manner and complained that one of them was left behind. Another traveller came there and counted them ten fellows, as all of them forgot to count themselves. A third man, a learned wise person was required to tell them that they were ten. This implies that only a wise preceptor can give proper guidance.

353. दशहरान्यायः

See पञ्चदशी, तृप्तिदीप, 23-28

Cf. प्रायशिक्त विवेक, पृ० 81.

The maxim tells that he who observes a vow on the tenth day of the bright half of Jyeṣṭha month, gets rid of all the sins. When many profits are gained with one act, this maxim is used.

354. दशानामेकादशन्यायः

This maxim tells us that it is possible to spend one rupee more that is eleven rupees if a person is willing to spend ten rupees. Or it also means that the expenditure on the eleventh person can be adjusted in the calculated expenditure of ten persons.

355. दामव्यालकटन्यायः

Ex. दामव्यालकटन्यायस्तस्मान्मा तेऽस्तु राघव।
भीमभासदृढन्यायो नित्यमस्तु तवानघ॥

—योगवसिष्ठ 4.34.35

This maxim is based on a legend. A demon called Śaṃbara created three demons called Dāma, Vyāla and Kaṭa, out of his magical power. They had the power of pounding down mountains like Meru with only the palms of their hands. But they were born in the category of mosquitos as a result of their ignorance. This shows that stupid fellows may attain high positions but ultimately their ignorance leads them to their ruin.

356. दारुपुरुषन्यायः

This maxim alludes the delusion in which a wooden figure of a man is mistaken to be a real man.

357. दिवातनचन्द्रन्यायः

The moon-light is bright and pleasant in the night but her light appears to be dim and lusterless in the day time. Referring to this phenomenon, the maxim conveys the idea that a man of less qualities or brilliance does not shine in the presence of a brilliant man.

358. दिवान्धन्यायः

The owl cannot see anything in the daylight. It hates the sun-light which is useful and beneficial to other beings. The maxim based on this fact, says that the mean persons dislike the good and virtuous persons.

359. दीपकलिकान्यायः

In this maxim kalikā signifies a flame, resembling a bud. Though small like a bud in the beginning,a flame can spread sufficient light everywhere. Similarly, a man who is young in age but great or big in merits, may have tremendous fame in the world.

360. दुर्जनगर्दभन्यायः

मलिनीकुर्वन्नर्जुनवर्त्म मदीभवति राधेयः।
यदि ताडनादि लभते तथापि तच्छील एव खलः॥

There are many common characteristics between an ass and a wicked man. Both of them are capable of amassing wealth and both of them become intoxicated by it. Both of them become excited in the month of Āṣāḍha and do not change their way of life, though they receive good thrashing.

361. दुर्जनमशकन्यायः

The maxim brings out the resemblance between a wicked person and a mosquito. Both of them attack the human beings and trouble them.

362. दूरस्थपर्वतन्यायः

The maxim tells that the mountains appear to be fascinating from a long distance only. If we go near them, all the big stones, valleys and dark forests are visible and make us frighten. They look pleasant from a distance only. So also, the persons appear to be good from a distance. The more one tries to go near them, the more he is disillusioned.

363. दूरस्थवनस्पतिकान्यायः

The maxim suggests that the two trees appear to be the same or one from a long distance. The difference between them is not grasped properly from a distance.

364. दुर्वामूलन्यायः

The roots of grass spread deep into the earth. They are not seen apparently but with the rainfall, the sprouts of little delicate green grass come up from the ground. The things may not be visible from outside but if their roots have gone deep down like the grass, they do not die. The maxim based on this phenomenon suggests that principles are too deep to be examined by their external appearance.

365. दृष्टिसृष्टिन्यायः

Ex. एवं दृष्टिसृष्टिन्यायेनास्मत्कल्पितोऽव्ययं वियदादिप्रपञ्चोऽस्मत्सुषुप्तौ लीयतेऽस्मत् प्रबोधे यथापूर्वं प्रादुर्भवति।

—सा० 918

The creator creates the world of sentient and insentient beings but all that world gets dissolved in the night of the creator i.e.Brahmā. It appears again when the day of Brahmā rises- All the creation is thus appearance and disappearance in the day and night of Brahmā.

366. देवताधिकरणन्यायः

Some scholars maintain that many scriptural statements describe the image of the deities. Actually. the image form is not natural. It is superimposed on deities. But it can be argued that though some statements underline the devotion to the deities, the implied meaning can be proved to be the real one, in accordance with the maxim of Devatādhikaraṇa.

367. देवदत्तशौर्यन्यायः

Devadatta's fame as a brave hero is limited to a particular town in which he is living. Others, living out side that town may not have any idea about his bravery. A person of heroic quality is recognized somewhere and sometime as a great hero and become famous.

368. देवदत्तहन्तृहतन्यायः

न हि अन्यस्यान्यसिद्धत्वादन्यस्य प्रादुर्भावो भवति।
न हि देवदत्तस्य हन्तरि हते देवदत्तस्य प्रादुर्भावो भवति।

—पतञ्जलि, व्याकरणमहाभाष्य, 1.1.57

This maxim is based on a small event. When Devadattal is killed, he cannot be rejuvenated, even though his assasins are arrested and given death sentence.

369. देवदत्तापुत्रन्यायः

When someone remarks that a particular person is the son of Devadatta, it also implies that he is the son of his wife also.The maxim says that the son belongs to both—the mother and the father but the father is given more importance, so his name is taken and not the name of the mother.

370. देवरन्यायः

A childless man may utilize the services of his brother or brother-in-law, to get a child from his wife. The maxim based on this idea, states that a man may go to any extreme to get his wish fulfilled.

371. देहकेशन्यायः

Cf. गोमयवृश्चिकन्यायः

The existence of the hair on the body is natural. Two things may not bear resemblance but they can be together. —सा० 891

372. देहलीदीपन्यायः

If a lamp is kept on the threshold. which is in between

the two rooms, the lamp light spreads in both the rooms.

This gives rise to a maxim and constitutes the basis of the figure of speech called 'Dīpaka', in which an object or its attribute illumines the entire sentence.

373. देहाधोमुखन्यायः

Cf. **आकाशपरिच्छन्नन्यायः**

A man suffering from rheumatic disease, hangs his head down. But when that disease (disappears) is cured, he becomes a normal man and sits erect. So also, the physical diseases from the body, disappear when their cause becomes extinct.

374. द्राविडप्राणायामन्यायः

The maxim refers to a practice, prevalent among the. Dravid people. While practising breath control (Prāṇāyāma), they hold the nose with the hand in a round about way instead of holding it directly from the front facing. This generally refers to the habit of some people who take a long, round about way of doing any work.

375. धनञ्जय न्यायः

Ex. निषेधमहिम्ना बाधितेऽपि द्वैते वाक्यजबोधस्य धनञ्जय-न्यायेन बाधकत्वोपपत्तेः।

यथाहुः नित्यबोधपरिपीडितं जगद् विभ्रमं नुदति वाक्यजा मतिः।

वासुदेवनिहतं धनञ्जयो हन्ति कौरवकुलं यथा पुनः॥

–रघुनाथ, लौकिकन्यायसाहस्त्रीयुद्धतः

This maxim indicates that a particular work can be repeated. Śrikṛṣṇa had already defeated the Kauravas in a divine manner but Arjuna did the same thing physically. See—**मयेवेते निहताः पूर्वमेवं निमित्तमात्रं भव सव्यसाचिन् ॥**

—भगवद्गीता XI.33

376. धनुर्गुणन्यायः

Ex. आजन्मतोऽतिकुटिलेऽपि जने महान्त-
स्त्वारोपयन्ति हि गुणं धनुषीव शूराः।

—सायण, लौकिकन्याय; सा० 896

The string of the bow is applied to the bow, only after bending it. The maxim based on this fact conveys that a good person may impose his qualities on a bad person also.

377. धान्यपलालन्यायः

Ex. (१) शास्त्राण्यधीत्य मेधावी ह्यभ्यस्य च पुनः पुनः।
परमं ब्रह्म विज्ञाय ह्युल्कावत्तान्यथोत्सृजेत्॥

(२) ग्रन्थमभ्यस्य मेधावी ज्ञानविज्ञानतत्परः।
पलालमिव धान्यार्थो त्यजेद्ग्रन्थमशेषतः॥

—ब्रह्मबिन्दूपनिषद् 14; पातञ्जलमहाभाष्य—1.2.39, 3.3.18; 3.4.2; 4.1.12

The maxim tells that while reading a text, one should take the essential thing from the text book and leave off unessential things, as one collects rice (or grain) and leaves off the chaff.

378. धारावाहिकबुद्धिन्यायः

Intellect is of the nature of determination. Owing to its working, many ideas enter and many disappear from the intellect of a person. Thus says the maxim, the ideas move in a manner of a continuously flowing course of the stream.

379. धूमाग्निन्यायः

This maxim refers to a famous statement in Nyāya, where there is smoke, there is fire. It also conveys the general truth that the smoke is the indicator of the fire. This invariable concomittance of two objects is called Vyāpti.

380. धेनुकिशोरन्यायः

Ex. जैमिनिमीमांसासूत्र VII.4.7.

The word 'Dhenu' means a cow. But the words like 'Asvadhenukishora' means a female horse. This maxim refers to some such rule about compounds.

381. नक्रन्यायः

नक्रः स्वस्थानमासाद्य गजेन्द्रमपि कर्षति।
स एव प्रच्युतः स्थानाच्छुनाऽपि परिभूयते।। —पञ्चतन्त्र 3.44

This maxim refers to a fact in life. A man who is firm in his position, is difficult to be unseated. An allegator, when it is firm in its area, it is very dangerous. But once it is displaced, even a dog can defeat it.

382. नटाङ्गनान्यायः

Ex. यथा नटानां स्त्रियो रङ्गगता यो यः पृच्छति
कस्य यूयं कस्य यूयमिति तं तं तव तवेत्याहुः।
एवं व्यञ्जनान्यपि यस्य यस्याचः कार्यमुच्यते
तं तं भजन्ते। —सा० 370

This maxim conveys that an actress who plays the role of a wife on the stage, says to the actors "she is his wife." She has to play the role of a wife despite those who play the role of the husband.

383. नदीसमुद्रन्यायः

Ex. यथा नद्य स्पन्दमानाः समुद्रेऽस्तं गच्छन्ति नामरूपे विहाय
तथा विद्वान्नामरूपाद्विमुक्तः परात्परं पुरुषमुपैति दिव्यम।।

Cf. **शकुनिसूत्रन्याय, शुद्धोदलवणन्याय, चौरापहार्यन्याय, पुंविषयन्याय, नानावृक्षरसन्याय**

—सा० 817, 818, 819, 820, 821, 822

As the river meets the ocean and forsakes its name and form, the individual self also merges with the . Brahman, leaving no sign of separate existence behind Similarly, a devotee gets merged in the supreme God. The dualists, however, maintain that the river and ocean are different. —सा० 818

384. नद्यम्बुवेगन्यायः

यथा नदीनां बहवोऽम्बुवेगाः समुद्रमेवाभिमुखा द्रवन्ति।
तथा तवामी नरलोकवीरा विशन्ति वाक्त्राण्याभिविज्वलन्ति॥

—श्रीमद्भगवद्गीता, XI.11, 28; सा० 370

This maxim maintains that the turbulent water of the river ultimately merges with the big ocean. In fact, all the worldly entities ultimately are dissolved in the ocean.

385. नरसिंहन्यायः

व्यक्ताव्यक्ता च संसृष्टिर्नरसिंहवदिष्यते।
चित्रवर्णवदन्यस्मिन्न्नानालङ्कार सङ्करे॥

—सरस्वतीकष्ठाभरणम्, पृ० 262

This maxim is used to describe a man who combines in himself terrific and mild qualities, as the man-lion incarnation of Lord Viṣṇu combined in himself the man and the lion.

386. नष्टाश्वदग्धरथन्यायः

(i) **स्थानेऽन्तरतमः** (1.1.50).

(ii) **नष्टाश्वदग्धरथन्यायेनं 'कर्मणा पितृलोक' इति श्रुतेः।**

—रामतीर्थ, वेदान्तसार टीका, पृ० 13

(i) सम्प्रयोगो वा नष्टाश्वरथदग्धवत्। तद्यथा नष्टाश्वदग्धरथ संप्रयोगो भवति। तद्यथा तवाश्वोनष्टो ममापि रथो दग्ध उभौ सम्प्रयुज्यावहे।

(ii) नष्टाश्वदग्धरथन्यायेन "कर्मणा पितृलोक" इति श्रुतेः–

–रामतीर्थ वेदान्तसार टीका, पृ० 13

There is a legend on which the maxim is based. Two persons were going in a (chariot cart). Unfortunately, the (chariot cart) of one of them was burnt by the fire near a village. The (horses\bulls) of another person died. Thus the (chariot cart) of one person and the bulls of the other remained. They put the (chariot cart) and the bulls together and proceeded further. This indicates that it is always beneficial to put the available things to use.

387. नसर्वत्रतुल्यत्वन्यायः

Ex. न च सर्वत्र तुल्यत्वं स्यात् प्रयोजनकर्मणाम्।
चलनेन त्वसि योद्धा प्रयुङ्क्ते छेदनं प्रति॥

सेनापतिस्तु वाचैव भृत्यानां विनियोजकः।
राजा सन्निधिमात्रेण विनियुङ्क्ते कदाचन॥

–श्लोकवार्तिक, आत्मवाद, 86, 87

The maxim tells that the action which may inspire a person to do something, will not be able to inspire some other person to do the same thing. The commander of the army may inspire the soldiers by his words or orders. A soldier may inspire others by using his sword, whereas the king's presence only is a source of inspiration to the soldiers. He only watches the work of his soldiers.

388. नसिप्रोतबलीवर्दन्यायः

Ex. यथा गावो नसि प्रोतास्तन्त्यां वद्धाश्च दामभिः।
वाक्तन्यां नामभिर्बद्धां वहन्ति बलिमीशितुः॥
—भागवत XII,12.41; सा० 592

A rope is put in the nostrils of a bull with which the owner controls it. The bull does the work of carrying burden. So also. says the maxim, men are controlled by such rein-like rope which is made of long fibres of Vedic injunctions about Varṇas and Āśramas. The senses are compared to a bull here.

389. नागोष्ट्रन्यायः

The Vedic sentence like "a camel was saved and a boa was killed", are found in the Vedas. Similar sentences indicate the unsublating nature of the self. They set aside the non-self entities and secure the immutability of the self.

390. नानावृक्षरसन्यायः

Cf. शकुनिसूत्रन्याय, नदीसमुद्रन्याय, चौरापहार्यन्यायः
यथा पक्षी च सूत्रं च नानावृक्षरसा यथा।
यथा नद्यः समुद्राश्च शुद्धोदलवणे यथा॥
चोरापहार्यो च यथा यथा पुंविषया अपि।
तथा जीवेश्वरौ भिन्नौ सर्वदैव विलक्षणौ॥
—माधवाचार्य, सर्वदर्शनसङ्ग्रह, पूर्णप्रज्ञदर्शन

The trees in a forest constitute a forest from the point of view of unity, but exist as separate trees from the distributory point of view. The maxim is employed by the followers of Madhva to point out the separate nature of the individual selves, though they are part and parcel of the Almighty only.

391. नान्तरीयकन्यायः

स्वरितात् संहितार्थामनुदात्तानाम्।

—Bhāṣya on P. I.2.39; सा० 619

A person fetches paddy. He removes chaff and other unwanted things and collects rice only for his food. The maxim exorts people to accept essential things and reject unessential, unwanted things.

392. नारिकेलतृणन्यायः

This maxim is used to illustrate some impossible incidents. It refers to the following conversation—

One person asked a calf—"Why did you climb the coconut tree"

Calf replied-"to eat grass."

Both the question and answer are impossible and silly.

393. नारिकेलफलाम्बुन्यायः

This maxim is related to a mystery. There is sweet cool water inside a coconut which has got a hard, strong tough cover outside. Equally mysterious is the phenomenon of the world which emerges from the Brahman. So is the case with the mysterious sojourns of Lakṣmī that is wealth or prosperity. Noone knows how it comes and how many days she remains.

394. नाविकन्यायः

If the boatsman is present but the boat is not there or if the boat is there but the boatsman is absent, there is no use of having either of them. Both the things are dependent on each other. The maxim suggests that when two things are dependent on each other, the absence of one renders the presence of the other useless or ineffective.

395. नासिकाङ्गुलिन्यायः

समस्तव्यस्ततामेवं सति व्याचक्षतेऽत्र ये।
कर्षन्ति नासिकाग्रेण कर्णमूलं सुखेन ते॥

—सुरेश्वर, बृहदारण्यक वार्तिक IV.3.1182

The maxim is related to some inpossible task like uprooting the origin of the ear with the tip of the nose.

396. निम्नगाप्रवाहन्यायः

Ex. कुर्वते कर्म भोगाय कर्म कर्तुं च भुञ्जते।
नद्यां कीटा इवावतीदावर्तान्तरमाशुं ते।
व्रजन्तो जन्मनो जन्म लभते नैव निर्वृतिम्।
सत्कर्मपरिपाकान्ते करुणानिधिनोदधृताः।
प्राप्य तीरतरुच्छायां विश्राम्यन्ति यथासुखम्॥

—लौकिकन्याय साहस्त्री; सा० 151

Once an insect was afloat in the current of a river. It could escape from one whirlpool but unfortunately it got involved in another whirlpool. Similarly, says the maxim, an individual cannot escape from the troubles of rebirth all the time.

397. निर्धनमनोरथन्यायः

उन्नम्योन्नम्य तत्रैव निर्धनानां मनोरथाः।
हृदयेष्वेव लीयन्ते विधवास्त्रीस्तनाविव॥

—लौकिकन्याय साहस्त्री; सा० 805

This maxim maintains that less the wealth a man has, the more are his longings.

398. निर्व्यापाराम्बष्ठन्यायः

This maxim says that an idle barber applies his razor

anywhere or on anything available nearby. If he comes across a cat, he cuts its head with his weapon and does not spare even a cat.

399. निवातस्थितदीपन्यायः

Ex. यथा दीपो निवातस्थो नेङ्गते सोपमा स्मृता।
योगिनो यतचित्तस्य युञ्जतो योगमात्मनः॥
—भगवद्गीता VI.19; सा० 637

A lamp burns steadily and slowly in a windless place. It neither flickers nor fades in quiet, windless place. Similarly the mind of a person never becomes fickle who observes perfect self control and tranquility—says the maxim.

400. निषादस्थपतिन्यायः

Niṣāda is an artisan, a carpenter in particular. In Mīmāṁsā and some Śāstras, the compound 'Niṣāda-sthapati' occurs. The Mimāṁsā writers opine that the compound is Karmdhāraya and not a Tatpuruṣa compound. The nature of the compound is also discussed in some commentaries of the Brahmasūtras. It shows that Karmadhāraya compound is more powerful than Ṣaṣṭhī Tatpuruṣa compound.

401. नीलेन्दीवरन्यायः

Cf. करिबृंहितन्यायः, करकङ्कणन्यायः, चंद्रज्योत्स्नान्यायः, गजघटान्यायः, वाजिमन्दुरान्यायः, मृगवागुरान्याय।
—सा० 209

In all these, generally the initial word is redundant, though there may be some reason for redundancy.

The word 'Indīvara' itself means blue lotus.

The word Nīla blue need not be added to it but sometime

such words are added with some purpose. In this case, it indicates that the lotus is not only blue but it is "very much blue".

402. नृपनापितपुत्रन्यायः

This maxim is based on a legend. Once a king ordered his barber to go around the city and find out a handsome boy. He came across many handsome boys but he thought that they were just like his own son. That boy was actually very black and ugly looking. He took his son to the king, thinking the king would like the boy. The king became furious. The barber argued and said that he could not find such a handsome boy in the entire three worlds. The king was convinced by the fact that one loves one's own possessions, however ugly they may be!

403. नौकाग्रकाकन्यायः

Once a crow was perching on the mast of a boat in the ocean. The ship or the boat started sailing. When the crow felt the movement of the ship, it was frightened and began to fly over the sea. But there was not a single tree where it could perch on and so it returned to the same mast again. So also,the individual self may transmigrate anywhere but it has firm basis in the Supreme Brahman.

404. नौनाविकन्यायः

This maxim is used to show the relation between the carrier and the carried. This is illustrated by the boat and the boatsman. Therefore. there is no fault of mutual dependence.

405. न्यगोधबीजन्यायः

Even a small seed of a banyan tree grows into a big

tree if it falls on a fertile land. The maxim indicates that a small thing grows into a huge size in favourable circumstances.

406. पङ्कप्रक्षालनयायः

(i) प्रक्षालनाद्धि पङ्कस्य दूरादस्पर्शनं वरम्।

—महाभारत, वनपर्व 2.49

The maxim says that it is better to avoid mud than to wash the feet when the feet get stuck up in the mud. Similarly, it is better to prevent any mishap by remaining cautious than to run for some devices to avoid the loss. Prevention is better than cure.

407. पङ्ग्वन्धन्यायः

Ex. पुरुषस्य दर्शनार्थं कैवल्यार्थं तथा प्रधानस्य।
पङ्ग्बन्धवदुभयोरपि संयोग स्तत्कृत॥

—सर्गः सङ्ख्यकारिका।

A blind and a crippled, lame man met each other. They wanted to proceed by the same way. Both of them hit upon a plan. The blind man took the lame man on his shoulder. who guided the blind person. With the help and co.operation of both of them, they were able to reach their goal. This co.operation of the two destitute persons is suggested by this maxim.

408. पञ्जरचालनन्यायः

यथैकपञ्जरवर्तिन एकादशपक्षिणः प्रत्येकं प्रतिनियतव्यापाराः सन्तः सम्भूयैकं पञ्जरं चालयन्ति,
एवमेकं शरीरवर्तिन एकादशप्राणाः प्रत्येकं प्रतिनियतवृत्तयः सन्तः सम्भूयैक प्राणाख्यां वृत्तिं प्रतिलप्स्यन्त इति।

—ब्रह्मसूत्र, शाङ्करभाष्य, 2.4.9

Eleven birds were caught in a cage. One bird was unable to lift the cage in spite of his hard efforts. But when the birds together applied their strength, they were able to lift the cage easily. On the same ground, the eleven Prāṇas in the body together carry on the task of one Prāṇa, though their functions are different. This maxim is based on this incident.

409. पञ्जरमुक्तपक्षिचालनन्यायः

Ex. बन्धुमुक्तस्योर्ध्वगमनं दृष्टं यथा पञ्जरमुक्तशुकस्य यथा वारिनिर्भिन्नपरिणतैरण्डबीजस्य, यथा वा दृढपङ्कलिप्त जलनिमज्जनप्रक्षीणपङ्कलेपशुष्कालाबूफलस्य।

—वेदान्तकल्पतरू परिमल, लौकिक न्याय सहस्त्री; सा० 9

When a bird escapes from the cage, it moves and freely goes up and up. Similarly, the liberated individual self moves freely and is liberated ultimately says the maxim.

410. पञ्जरस्थसिंहन्यायः

Cf. **सलिलादग्निरुत्थितन्यायः**

स्नेहतन्तुमयैः पाशैर्बद्धः सन्तानरज्जुभिः।
पञ्जरस्थो यथा सिंहः समर्थोऽपि वशीकृतः॥

—लौकिकन्याय साहस्त्री; सा० 937

Even a lion, caught in a cage, is unable to move freely according to its will. Similarly, a man ensnared in a web of affection and tied by the rope of love for the children, is unable to do anything at his will.

411. पटकुटीरन्यायः

When there is sufficient cloth at our disposal, we can make a (cotton cloth) cottage or a (cotton cloth) tent out of it. The maxim based on this observation, shows that any task can be accomplished when adequate material is available.

412. पतङ्गदीपकन्यायः

The glow worm pounces on the flame of a burning

lamp, out of extreme love and affection, as it were. It really embraces death. Even then other glow worms continue to jump in the flames. The maxim shows that excessive love may endanger their lives. —सा० 326

413. पतिंवरान्यायः

In the Svayamvara function, the lady chooses her husband. (The bride chooses the bridegroom) according to her choice. So also, a man maintains contacts or good relationship with an affectionate person only.

414. पत्रफलन्यायः

There are leaves and sometimes fruits also on the tree. The leaves of the tree fade away and fall down on the ground. But by the falling of the leaves, the fruits are not spoiled. Similarly, a few men may have some defect or drawback, but it does not mean that all men are full of defects. This is what the maxim wants to suggest.

415. पथिकसर्पमारणन्यायः

Once a person saw a serpent, entering his house. The man was frightened and wanted to kill it. But he was in a dilemma and was puzzled because had he killed it, it would have resulted in a sin and if he kept quiet, the danger arising out of the serpent would have been unmitigated. He thought upon a device. He requested a passer-by to kill the serpent, so that the possible sin and the danger arising out of the serpent, would accrue to that passer by-instead of him. The maxim suggests that everyone in this world wants to save his life by hook or by crook.

416. पदातिन्यायः

Ex. ऋजुना पथा चलन्नपि हनने वक्रां गतिं कलयन्।
बुद्धिबलाख्यं क्रीडन् पदातिरिव दुर्जनो ज्ञेयः।

–लौकिकन्याय साहस्री; सा० 970

In the game of chess, a soldier piece generally moves one square straight but it can move slantingly or crookedly, if there is any chance of killing the opposite piece. The maxim can be applied to a wicked person who appears to move in a straight manner but may take crooked turn to kill somebody.

417. पद्मपत्रस्थिततोयन्यायः

Ex. (i) **पद्मपत्रस्थितं तोयं धत्ते मुक्ताफलश्रियम्।**
महाजनस्य सम्पर्कः कस्य नोन्नतिकारकः।।

—पञ्चतन्त्र 3.59

(ii) **मुक्ताकारतया तदेव नलिनीपत्र स्थितं राजते।**

—भर्तृहरि, नीतिशतक 58

(iii) **लिप्यते न स पापेन पद्मपत्रमिवाम्भसि।**

—भगवद्गीता 5-10; सा० 807

This maxim is based on the phenomenon of some water drops on a lotus-leaf. These water-drops do not last for a long time on the lotus leaf. They suggest the following points:—

(1) All creation is transitory.

(2) The company of the great, though temporary, is always benevolent. The water-drops on the lotus leaf, though temporary, shine like pearls so long as they remain on the leaf.

(3) All worldly contacts are momentary. Similarly a man of well balanced intellect or a man of mental and physical control lives in the world with complete detachment.

418. पनसोदुम्बरादिवदितिन्यायः

The maxim refers to a natural phenomenon. Generally,

the flowering period indicates that the fruit is not far. But pregnancy may take place even without the appearance of flower (maturity), as is the case with Udumbara tree or a jackfruit tree. We never see the flower of these trees but (they bear fruits without flowering) we see their fruits only.

—सा० 554

419. पयोमुखविषकुम्भन्यायः

Cf. **गोमुख व्याघ्रन्यायः** See—हितोपदेश, मित्रलाभ, 74

A jar is filled with poison but milk or a vessel full of milk is kept on the top or at the opening of the jar. Similarly, some men speak gently or lovingly but they may carry poison (are wicked) in their heart—says the maxim.

420. पराह्णच्छायान्यायः

Ex. **आरम्भगुर्वी क्षयिणी क्रमेण**
लघ्वी पुरा वृद्धिमती च पश्चात्।
दिनस्य पूर्वार्धपराधीभिन्ना
छायेव मैत्री खलु सज्जनानाम्।

—भर्तृहरि, नीतिशतक, 47

The length of a shadow of a thing is less in the earlier part of the day; while it is longer in the later part of the day. It is short in the afternoon but gradually it increases in the latter part of the day. The maxim opines that the friendship with the good people is longer and stable after some days though it seems shorter in the early days.

In contrast to this, the friendship with the wicked appears to be longer or close in the beginning but becomes shorter or less as the time passes.

421. परिशेषन्यायः

The maxim indicates the method of calculation on the basis of remainder. Suppose ten people (men and women together) are standing at one place. If it is reliably told that there are four men, then it is clear that the remaining six are women by the law of remainder.

422. पर्जन्यन्यायः

Ex. (1) **कृतकारि खल्वपि शास्त्रं पर्जन्यवत्। तद्यथा पर्जन्यो यावदूनं च पूर्णं च सर्वत्राभिवर्षति।**

—महाभाष्य, अष्टाध्यायी 1.2.9; 6.1.189

(2) **प्रकृत्यादिविभागकल्पनावस्तु लक्ष्येषु सामान्य विशेषरूपाणां लक्षणानां पर्जन्यवत्सकृदेव प्रवृत्तौ बहूनां शब्दानामनुशासनोपलम्भाच्च।**

—सर्वदर्शनसङ्ग्रह, पाणिनिप्रकरण

This maxim is based on the fact that the rain falls equally everywhere, whether water accumulates at a particular place or not. The rain falls with equal quantity of water at all places. This maxim is also applied to the functioning of the Almighty. The grace of God is uniformly bestowed on all beings. But its effects are seen diversely, owing to the Karmas (past deeds) of the recepients, as the rain-water, fallen on the fertile land, helps to germinate the seeds but becomes ineffective when fallen on the barren land.

Cf. ब्रह्मसूत्र, शाङ्करभाष्य, II.1.34

423. पर्णमयीन्यायः

Cf. **गोदोहनन्याय**

See—भामतीटीका, शाङ्करभाष्य, ब्रह्मसूत्र 3.3

The ladles to be used at the time of sacrificial rites, are made of palāśa or parṇa tree. That is its speciality.

424. पर्वताधित्यकान्यायः

Cf. करकङ्कणन्यायः, गजघटान्यायः

The word Adhityakā means the plain land on the top of the mountain. So, affixing of the word 'Parvata' is redundant. But as similar maxims show that there must be some purpose for adding the apparently redundant word. Cf. उपत्यकाद्रेशसन्ना भूमिउर्ध्वमाधित्यका अमर०

425. पवनताडनन्यायः

Cf. गगनरोमन्थन्यायः

This maxim is used to point out the futility of efforts like striking the air (wind).

426. पाटच्चरयामिकन्यायः

A thief steals away everything from a house. What is the use of appointing a secuity guard after that event? The maxim indicates the futility of such precautions after the event.

427. पात्रेसंमितन्यायः

Some people run away when they are given some work. But they rush back if they are likely to get some food.The maxim exposes such opportunists. He is a treacherous fellow who appears only at the time of meals and not at the time of work.

428. पादप्रसारिकान्यायः

Ex. एतत्सर्वमनालोच्य कृत्वा पादप्रसारिकाम्।
विवेकचक्षुः संमील्य स्वपन्ति ननु जन्तवः॥
ततो विषादमापन्नः सर्वकर्मपराङ्मुखः।
स्थितोऽहं मौनमालम्ब्य कृत्वा पादप्रसारिकाम्॥

(1) उपमितिभवप्रपञ्चकथा, पृ० 789, 909, (2) न्यायमञ्जरी, पृ० 133, 121, 504 (3) खण्डनखण्डखाद्य, पृ० 31.

If a person is offered some space, just to stretch his legs, he cunningly, tries to stretch his whole body and wants to occupy as much space as possible. This type of conduct is described by this maxim. Other meaning of the maxim is also possible. A man sticks to his aim or purpose despite his failure and even if there are is no chance of future success also.

429. पारिषदन्यायः

The maxim is applied to a peculiar type of behaviour in a meeting.

(i) Even if one man works at the meeting, it is supposed that all those concerned have extended their co-operation.

(ii) One member only is arguing about a certain subject in the meeting. It is supposed that those who support or those who oppose the argument, are the members of the meeting.

430. पाषाणेष्टकान्यायः

This maxim conveys the idea that though two things appear to be alike, some difference does exist between the two, as there is some difference in softness or hardness between a brick and a stone. Though both are hard, a brick is softer than a stone.

431. पिङ्गलाजपन्यायः

This maxim describes a hypocritical man, by citing the instance of a harlot called Pingalā who tried to deceive a rich person by assuming the form of a Yoginī.

432. पिण्डहित्वाकरंलेढीति न्यायः

When a selfish person keeps the lump of food aside and asks a hungry man to lick his hand to which some particles of food are sticking, this maxim has its scope. It also indicates enjoying low type of joy, in preference to the higher one of the realization of the supreme self.

433. पितापुत्रन्यायः

This maxim informs that one person may be both a father and a son at the same time. He has to assume two positions at a time.

434. पित्रनुसृतस्तनन्धयन्यायः

Ex. कृतकृत्यस्य तत्त्वविदोऽतत्त्वविदुद्धारातिरिक्तकर्तव्यभावाद्यथा तदुद्धारः स्यात्तथा कर्तव्यम् । सुरेन्द्रादिपूज्येनापि विदुषा पित्रनुसृतस्तनन्धयन्यायेनाज्ञोऽनुसर्तव्यः। तैर्निन्द्यमानोऽपि देहस्य निन्द्यत्वमात्मनोऽवाङ्मनसगम्यत्वं जानन्नोद्विजेत्। किन्तु, प्रस्तुत तच्चेष्टानुसारेण स्वयमप्याचरेत।

This maxim describes a man of Brahma realization who behaves in a very simple, innocent manner like a father, imitating his son in his innocence and simplicity.

435. पिपीलिकान्यायः–पिपीलिकागतिन्यायः

This maxim lauds the spirit of endeavour. An ant for example, tries patiently and strenuously to climb the tree to taste a fruit. Similarly, the maxim states that a man can also accomplish difficult tasks by endeavouring patiently. Even to enjoy Brahma-realization patience of an ant is required.

436. पिपीलिकापन्नगन्यायः

The ants prepare an ant hill. But the serpents live in it

The maxim is based on the situation in which one person strives to do something but somebody else enjoys the fruit of it.

437. पिष्टपेषणन्यायः

Cf. **मृतमारणन्याय, जलताडनन्याय, अरण्यरोदनन्याय श्वपुच्छोन्नामनन्याय।**

—सा०, पृ० 115-116

To grind the flour which is already ground. This is the meaning of the maxim which suggests the habit of unnecessary repetition of work.

—सा० 301

438. पीलुपत्रफलन्यायः

The leaves of the Pilu tree are pungent but the fruits of the same tree are very sweet. Taking clue from this, the maxim suggests some discrepancies especially in the case of prattlings of a foolish fellow. This foolish fellow speaks in contradictory terms.

—सा० 668

439. पुत्रान्तरकाङ्क्षणीन्यायः

यो ध्रुवाणि परित्यज्य ध्रुवाणि निषेवते।
ध्रुवं तस्य निनष्टं स्यादध्रुवं नष्टमेव हि॥

—हितोपदेश, मित्रलाभ 184

The maxim is based on a legend of a woman who had one son but was eager to have one more son. Not satisfied with one son, she began to pray God for another son. She approached a lady who was a hypocrite. That lady advised her to sacrifice her first son for getting a second son. Having come to know this, an old lady advised her not to believe that wretched lady because if she did not get another son, she would loose the first son also. That would lead to total despair. The maxim suggests that one who runs after imaginery benefits, abandoning the one in hand, comes to ruin.

440. पुराणवैराग्यन्यायः

Cf. श्मशानवैराग्यन्याय

This maxim is concerned with a man of temporary detachment. So long as a person hears the stories or discourses on Purāṇas, he feels detachment towards the worldly happiness and temporary existence in the world. He becomes a totally detached person as long as he hears the discourses. But that feeling of detachment disappears and he plunges in the worldly affairs afterwards. A person's feeling of detachment is too weak to last for a long time.

441. पुरुषकेशलोमन्यायः

A man has hair on his body and they develop and grow on (his) body. This maxim says that as the body hair grows in a person's body, this empirical world also arises from the Supreme Reality.

–सा० 769

442. पुंविषयन्यायः

Cf. शकुनिसूत्रन्याय, नदीसमुद्रन्याय, शुद्धोदलवणन्याय, नानावृक्षरसन्याय इ.

Ex. यथा पक्षी च सूत्रं च नानावृक्षरसा यथा।
यथा नद्यः समुद्राश्च शुद्धोदलवणे यथा।
चोरायहार्यौ च यथा तथा पुंविषयावपि।
तथा जीवेश्वरौ भिन्नौ सर्वदैव त्रिंलक्षणौ॥

–लौकिकन्याय साहस्त्री; सा० 817-822

The maxim refers to an opinion of the dualist, that the individual self and the God are quite different from each other, though they are grammatically in the same masculine gender.

443. पुष्करपलाशन्यायः

Ex. (1) ज्ञानाग्निः सर्वकर्माणि भस्मासात् कुरुते यथा।

—भगवद्गीता, 4.37

(2) लिप्यते न स पापेन पद्मपत्रमिवाम्भसा॥

—भगवद्गीता, 5.10

The maxim describes the nature of an enlightened person. Just as the water-drops fallen on the lotus leaves, do not last long, the action (Karma) does not cling to an enlightened person. The fire of knowledge burns down all actions.

444. पुष्टलगुडन्यायः

If a stick is thrown at a dog in a group of dogs. it not only hits the particular dog but other dogs also. The maxim implies that arguments advanced to refute one point, refute some other points also.

445. पुष्पवन्तोपकारकन्यायः

The sun and the moon possess lustre (Puṣpa). Those two offer their lustre to the other planets which happen to pass within their orbit and thus oblige them. Similarly, says the maxim that the great men oblige men who come in their contact.

446. पूतिकूष्माण्डन्यायः

A pumpkin produced in a dirty place is not supposed to be liked by everybody. It is not good for eating. Everyone does not like to eat it. The maxim states that a thing like a pumpkin, grown in bad surroundings is not liked by the people. —सा० 774

447. पूर्णघटन्यायः

रिक्तः सर्वो भवति हि लघुः पूर्णता गौरनाय।

—मेघदूत, पूर्वमेघ 20

The maxim avers that the water in a pitcher which is full of water never shakes. Similarly, a man, having deep knowledge never complains. He is always quiet and stable. A man having perfect knowledge and perfect enlightenment never trembles like a pitcher which is completely filled with water.

448. पूर्वाह्नच्छायान्यायः

Ex. दिनस्य पूर्वाधपरार्धभिन्ना छायेव मैत्री खलसज्जनानाम्।

—भर्तृहरि, नीतिशतक, 49.

The maxim compares the friendship of the wicked man with the morning shadow, which is the longest in the beginning but gradually reduces as the time passes by. The company with the wicked person is also very thick and intimate at the beginning but goes on declining day by day. The friendship with the good people is quite opposite.

449. पृथिव्योषधिन्यायः

Ex. यथोर्णनाभिः सृजते गृह्णते च
यथा पृथिव्यामोषधयः सम्भवन्ति।
यथा सतः पुरुषात् केशलोमानि
तथाऽक्षरात्सम्भवतीह विश्वम्।।

—मुण्डकोपनिषद् 1.1.7; सा० 768

The maxim states that just as herbs take their rise from the earth, the world also arises from the Brahman.

450. पृष्टाकोटिन्यायः

अथ सिद्धे दुरिते का तत्सङ्ख्येति प्रायश्चित्तकदम्बाद्युक्तगणना लिख्यते। सा च पृष्टाकोटि न्यायेन वक्तुमशक्याऽपि स्थूलोपाधि विषयत्वेनोच्यते।

–धर्मनिबन्ध, लौकिकन्याय साहस्त्री; सा० 258

The maxim tells that even a great scholar cannot give answers to all the questions, asked. He may not be able to answer every question put to him but he can definitely give some information pertaining to the question put to him. Even a scholar has his limitations.

–सा० 587

451. पृष्ठताडनाद्दन्तभङ्गन्यायः

The maxim refers to a senseless, implausible remark of a person that the teeth of a certain person were broken and fell down when somebody bet him at his back.

452. प्रतिनिधिन्यायः (प्रतिनिधानन्याय)

Ex. भोजनलोपेऽप्यद्भिर्वाऽन्येन वा द्रव्येणाविरुद्धेनप्रतिनिधानन्यायेन प्राणाग्निहोत्रस्यानुष्ठानमिति।

–ब्रह्मसूत्र, शाङ्करभाष्य, 3.3.40

The maxim incorporates a universal practice of any group of people having a representative of them, to deal with their problems.

453. प्रतिबिम्बन्यायः

When a thing shakes, its reflection also seems to be shaken. This is the meaning of this maxim.

454. प्रत्यासत्तिन्यायः

The maxim maintains that big tasks can be accomplished

by keeping contact or by remaining in the company of the prominent persons.

455. प्रदीपन्यायः

कश्चिदेकदेशस्थः सर्वं शास्त्रमभिज्वलयति, यथा प्रदीपः।
सुप्रज्वलित एकदेशस्थः सर्वं वेश्माभिज्वलयति॥

एकदेशस्थिता शास्त्रभवने याति दीयताम्।
परितो व्यापतां भाषां परिभाषां प्रचक्षते॥

—नागेश उद्योत, पृ० 8

This maxim takes into consideration the main characteristic of a lamp—.

(1) The wick, oil and fire which are quite different, come together to do the pious work of producing and giving light to the people.

(2) The lamp is kept in one place only but it gives light upto a long distance. The maxim suggests that even contradictory things can give good result if they come together.

The three types of Adhikarīs are compared with the three constituents of the lamp.

456. प्रधानमललनिबर्हणन्यायः

Ex. (एतेन सर्वे व्याख्याता—) अतः प्रधानमल्लनिबर्हण-न्यायेनातिदिशति। एतेन प्रधानकारणवादप्रतिषेधन्यायकलापेन सर्वेऽपवादिकारणवादा अपि प्रतिषिद्धतया व्याख्याता वेदितव्याः।

—ब्रह्मसूत्र, शाङ्करभाष्य 1.4.28; सा० 244

If a strong prominent wrestler is defeated, it becomes easy to defeat other wrestlers who are less powerful than the defeated one. On this ground only, the Advaita

Vedantins try to rebut the Sāṁkhya doctrine, as they were relatively stronger.

457. प्रपाणकरन्याय (पानकरसन्याय)

सकलसहृदयसंवादभाजा साधारण्येन स्वाकार इवाभिन्नोऽपि गोचरीकृतश्चर्व्यमाणतैकप्राणो विभावादिजीविव्यवधिः पानकरसन्यायेन चार्ण्यमाणः . . . .ब्रह्मस्वादमिवानुभावयन् अलौकिकचमत्कारकारी शृङ्गारादिको रसः।

—काव्यप्रकाश उल्लास 4, पृ० 93

In a particular drink (Pānaka), different things like sugar, pepper, ginger . are added which gives a peculiar taste to the drink, which is different from the individual substances added to it. The maxim states that the unified taste of all these ingredients gives a different sweet taste.

458. प्रपामेलनन्यायः

यथा काष्ठं च काष्ठं च समेयातां महोदधौ।
समेत्य च व्यपेयातां तद्वज्जीवसमागमः॥ —सा० 868

—बाल्मीकिरामायण, अयोध्याकाण्ड, 105-25

Many travellers come to drink water at a water-place (Prapā). They drink water and proceed further. They come together only for a few moments and are separated again like the two logs of wood coming near each other in the vast ocean. Similarly, human beings in this world come in contact with one another only to be separated like the two logs of wood in the ocean.

459. प्रभातमेघन्यायः

The morning clouds rarely shower. Similarly even good persons do not extend any help if approached at odd time, says the maxim.

460. प्रभुभृत्यन्यायः

The maxim declares that affection shown by the master for his servant and the devotion of the servant for his master, indicate mutual faith.

461. प्रमदान्यायः

A beautiful lady gives delight to her husband. Another person who sees her, is dismayed as he does not have a similarly beautiful wife. Her cowife, if he has any, creates further envy in her. This shows that various types of feelings are nursed by different persons about one person only.

—सा० 928

462. प्रवत्स्यद्भर्तृकान्यायः

A lady sees that her husband is going on a journey. Imagining the future pain of separation, she cries before him and tries to cancel his journey as she is unable to bear the pangs of separation.

463. प्रसक्तप्रतिषेधन्यायः

(1) प्रसज्य प्रसक्ति सम्पाद्यारोप्येति यावत्प्रतिषेघः। अत्यन्ताभावे प्रसक्तं हि प्रतिविध्यत इति न्यायेन आरोपितं प्रसङ्गस्यैव निषेधः। तेन वायौ रूपं नास्ति, इत्यादावपि वायौ रूपारोपं कृत्वैव निषेधो नञा बोध्यत, इति विवेकः।

—मीमांसान्यायकोश, पृ० 252.

Where prohibition or negation is principal, it is Prasajya Pratiṣedha. In other cases it is called Paryudāsa. The prohibition in the case of the former one pertains to a verb while in the case of the latter, it is connected with some noun.

464. प्रसक्तानुप्रसक्तन्यायः

A man obliges his friend by doing some good to him Any other person, set out for different work, may also be benefitted by the first person.

465. प्रसूतिवैराग्यन्यायः

When a pregnant lady, woefully cries just before delivery, determines not to have any contact with the husband. She develops detachment for sex and pregnancy. But once the baby is born and days pass on, she begins to aspire for another issue, forgetting the erstwhile unbearable pain. The maxim suggests that feigned, temporary detachment does not last long.

466. प्रासादवासिन्यायः

The maxim tells that a man lives in the upper apartments or in the lower apartments of a mansion. But he remains in the same mansion only. This finds its place in some rules of Sanskrit grammar. Just as some people live in palace, some on the ground and some on both ground and in big mansions. Similarly some letters in grammar are uttered from the mouth, some from the nose and some from both mouth and nose. These differences are made clear by this maxim.

467. प्लवङ्गगतिन्यायः

A monkey jumps once, twice, thrice and catches the fruit of the tree. Similarly, declares the maxim that a mediocre person who is slightly superior to the ignorant one, can acquire spiritual knowledge from the preceptor by virtue of his pure mindedness or Saṁskaras.

468. फलवत्सहकारन्यायः

आम्रे फलार्थे निर्मिते छायागन्धे अनुत्पद्यते। एवं धर्मे चर्यमाणे अर्थादयोऽनूत्पद्यन्ते। —सा० 4

A mango tree bends low when it is loaded with fruits. It regales those who seek refuge in it and regales them even by offering them sweet fruits and fragrance. Similarly, the deity whom we worship bestows many benefits on the worshippers like us but also offers many other benefits.

469. बकबन्धनन्यायः

Once a person wanted to catch a crane. He pelted a ball of butter on the head of it. After some time, the butter started melting and the liquid entered into the eyes of the crane. It became easy for the person to catch the bird because it could not see anything. The maxim points out that the people adopt difficult ways unnecessarily when the things can be attained easily.

470. बकवृत्तिन्यायः

A crane is accustomed to feign meditation and keeps its eye on the fish below. It catches the fish as soon as it comes near it. Its meditation is mere hypocracy. The maxim, with the example of the crane, hints at a person who acts like a hypocrite.

471. बधिरकर्णन्यायः

Cf. उधरवृष्टिन्याय, अन्धदर्पणन्याय, बधिरशङ्खनादन्याय

—लौकिकसाहस्त्री, पृ० 115, 116

This maxim is applied to certain futile actions like whispering some secret information in the ears of a deaf man. That effort of speaking slowly or loudly is of no use. Similar maxims, seventeen in number are enumented in सा० (pp. 115, 116)

472. बहुच्छिद्रघटप्रदीपन्यायः

नानच्छिद्रघटोदरस्थितमहादीपप्रभाभास्वरं
ज्ञानं यस्य तु चक्षुरादिकरणद्वारा बहिः स्पन्दते।

जानामीति तमेव भान्तमनुभात्येतत् समस्तं जगत्
तस्मै श्रीगुरुमूर्तये नम इदं श्रीदक्षिणामूर्तये॥

—दक्षिणामूर्तिस्तोत्र, शंकराचार्यकृत; सा० 363

If a lamp is kept within a jar which has many holes, the light of the lamp spreads out of all the holes and makes the space bright with its light. Similarly, the intellect permeates the external objects through the nine apertures of the body.

473. बहुराजकपुरन्यायः

वाक्यक्षुः श्रोत्रमुख्यानि प्रेरयेत् करणानि कः।
ईश्वरश्चेत् किमेकोऽसौ बाहवोऽभी॥
प्रवर्त्यानामनन्तत्वाद् वैलक्षण्याच्च नैकता।
नैकमत्यं बहुत्वे स्याद् बहुराजकदेशवत्॥

—अनुभूतिप्रकाश, 12.13; सा० 191

If many kings live in a town, they cannot maintain unity among themselves and the subjects will suffer. Taking this into account, the maxim says-many sense organs in the body put the entire body to troubles, as their functions are quite different. No perception will be proper if the organs start functioning simultaneously, when the eye is observing something particularly.

474. बहुवल्लभन्यायः

The maxim suggests that a person cannot satisfy any master if he has many masters, as a lady cannot satisfy any husband if she has many husbands.

475. बहुवृकाकृष्टन्यायः

If a deer is caught by many wolves, they try to tear off various limbs of its body at their will and spoil the entire body of the deer. The maxim says that unplanned efforts are not very fruitful. —सा० 18

476. बहुसपत्नीकन्यायः

Ex. जिह्वैकतोऽमुमपकर्षति कर्हि तर्षा
शिश्नोऽन्यतस्त्वगुदर श्रवणं कुतश्चित्।
घ्राणोऽन्यतश्चपल दकं क्व च कर्मशक्तिर्बह्व्यः
सपत्न्य इव गेहपति लुनन्ति। —भागवत

If a man has many wives, he cannot give sexual joy to all at a time. Similarly the maxim observes that a person cannot satisfy different sense organs.

477. बह्वनुग्रहन्यायः

बहूनामप्यसाराणां मेलनं कार्यसाधकम्।
तृणैः सम्पाद्यते रज्जुर्यथा नागोऽपि बध्यते।।

—सुभाषित

The maxim lauds the combined strength of different individuals which is produced after their coming together. The blades of grass are weak but when they are woven together into a rope, even a big elephant can be tied with it and controlled.

478. बह्वनुसरणन्यायः

This maxim tells that many a time it is advisable to follow the views of many people.

479. बाणोष्ट्रीन्यायः

The maxim states that the prohibitory injunctions or sentences protect the self and annul the non-self. This is supported by an event. Once a boa encircled a female camel. On seeing this, an archer shot an arrow at the boa and saved the female camel.

—सा० 104

480. बादरायणसम्बन्धन्यायः

अस्माकं बदरीचक्रं युष्माकं बदरीतरुः।
बादरायणसम्बन्धो यूयं यूयं वयं वयम्॥ (लोकोक्तिः)

This maxim speaks about the habit of some person who tries to establish some far fetched relation with somebody (with a view to derive some advantage from him). Any man who has a wheel made of Badara wood in his house, establishes relation with somebody, simply because he had planted a Badara tree in his (house) garden. Once two persons accidently met each other at one place. One person said to the other. "You have a Bādarī tree in your house. The wheels of my cart are also made of Bādarī wood. So we are related and there is Bādarāyaṇa (i.e. irrational, arbitrary) relation between us". This is how absolutely unrelated persons try to establish fantastic relation with other for their selfish end. —सा० 491

481. बिडालविण्मोचनन्यायः

The cat scratches the ground to creat a small ditch and then passes urine in it. It closes the ditch with the surrounding loose earth when the work of passing urine is over. The maxim cites the example of the cat suggesting that one should do away with the temporary arrangement, when the work is over.

482. बिल्वखल्वाटन्यायः

खल्वाटो दिवसेश्वरस्य किरणैः सन्तापितो मस्तके
वाञ्छन् देशमनातपं विधिवशाद् बिल्वस्य मूलं गतः।
तत्राप्यस्य महत्फलेन पतता भग्नं सशब्दं शिरः
प्रायो गच्छति यत्र भाग्यरहितस्तत्रैव यान्त्यापदः॥

—भर्तृहरि, नीतिशतक, सा० 113

The maxim refers to some unfortunate plight of a person. A bald-headed man was travelling from a forest. He was tired. So he stood under the shade of a Bilva tree to take rest. Unfortunately, a ripe Bilva fruit fell on his head and his head was broken. An unfortunate person has to face trouble and difficulty wherever he goes. His misfortune does not leave him anywhere.

483. बिल्ववर्तिगोधान्यायः

The maxim maintains that the doctrine propounded by the rival persons cannot be refuted, if the doctrine is not known perfectly, with its pros and cons. A Godhā, a big lizard, lives in a hole but it is not seen always living in a hole. So it cannot be taken as a differentiating feature, owing to the ignorance of its behavioural characteristic.

484. बिल्वविभजनन्यायः

The maxim condemns the practice of giving one's views about unknown matters, like trying to know about a Bilva fruit (about which nothing is known earlier), only by breaking it.

485. बीजवृक्षन्यायः

The maxim tells that though a seed gives rise to a sprout, the sprout also grows into a tree which gives rise to seed and sprout too. Both are beginningless and there is no order or priority between a seed and a sprout.

486 बीजाङ्कुरन्यायः

It is difficult to answer the question— "Which is earlier, seed or tree? Does a seed come out of the tree or does the tree arise out of the seed"? Actually, their relation is beginningless. Both of them serve as cause of each other. The maxim tells that it is possible to establish priority of one over the other. Their relation is beginningless.

487. ब्राह्मणग्रामन्यायः

Cf. **मल्लग्रामन्यायः**

Many kinds of people live in a town. There are Brāhmaṇas as well as other types of people also. But if the number of Brāhmaṇa inhabitants is more, then the town will be known as the Brāhmaṇa town. The maxim shows that the majority of the type of people is the main criteria for considering the name of the town.

—सा० 27

488. ब्राह्मणपरिव्राजकन्यायः

Ex. Cf.**ब्राह्मणश्रमणन्यायः** शाबरभाष्य, मीमांसासूत्र-2.1.43

इतो ब्राह्मणा भोज्यन्तामितः परिव्राजका इति।

—सा० 203; ब्रह्मसूत्र, शाङ्करभाष्य 1.4.16; 2.3.15; 3.1.11

The word Brāhmaṇa is a common word, denoting the Brāhmaṇa caste. But when the word mendicant-Parivrājaka comes as the final word in a compound with the word 'Brāhmaṇa', it means a Brāhmaṇa other than a mendicant. In order to differentiate between the Brāhmaṇas and the mendicants, the compound means the mendicants other than the Brāhmaṇas, as some mendicants are likely to be Brāhmaṇas by caste.

489. ब्राह्मणवसिष्ठन्यायः

Cf. **तक्रकौण्डिन्यन्यायः**

The sentence Brāhmaṇa has come and Vasiṣṭha has

also come means that Vasiṣṭha who is a Brāhmaṇa has come. The term Brāhmaṇa in the former part of the sentence sets aside other special characteristics. Therefore, the term Brāhmaṇa is used. This maxim is utilized in the explanation of the Paṇinian Sūtra "Halantyam".

490. ब्राह्मश्रमणन्यायः

Cf. गोबलीवर्दन्यायः

यः पूर्वं क्वापि वाक्यार्थे अलङ्कारभावमुपमादिरूपतया अन्वभूत्, इदानीं त्वजलङ्काररूप एव, अन्यत्र गुणीभावभावात्।

स पूर्वप्रत्यभिज्ञानबलात् अलङ्कारध्वनिरिति व्यपदिश्यते ब्राह्मणश्रमणन्यायेन। —सा० 168

A brāhmaṇa embraces Buddhism and becomes a Bhikṣu or a Śramaṇaka. Nevertheless, he is referred to as a Brāhmaṇa owing to his previous state. This maxim is used in the Sāhitya śāstra works to explain the figure of speech called Vyatireka Alaṁkāra.

491. भद्राघटन्यायः

A person called Bhadra served a Yakṣa ardently. As a result of it, he got a Bhadraghaṭa from the Yakṣa which yielded all the desires. Once he served rich delicious food to his relatives and friends. They, obviously, wanted to know the reason behind his sudden prosperity. Once in an intoxicated mood, he kept that jar on his head and began to saunter here and there. Unfortunately, that Bhadraghaṭa fell down from his head and broke into pieces. The maxim, through this example, conveys that an arrogant and an unlucky person cannot retain his affluence.

492. भर्छुन्यायः

Cf. भैरवप्रियन्यायः

Once a king assigned the task of controlling the robbers to his minister called Bharchu. He finished the work successfully but stayed back to complete his job. The persons who were jealous of him, spread the rumour that Bharchu was killed in an encounter with the robbers. So another person was appointed as the minister.Bharchu wanted to return to his capital but he got the news of the appointment of another minister. He was disgusted and remained in the forest. When the enemy came to know about it, they told the king that he had become a goblin.

This incident gives rise to an opinion that once a person is defamed, he remains in that condition only.

—सा० 394

493. भल्लूककम्बलभ्रान्तिन्यायः

This maxim is based on an event. Once a big tree was floating on the current of a river. A bear was also being carried along with it. Thinking that it is some blanket, two persons jumped in the current of water to catch it. But, alas, the bear pounced on them and killed both of them. The maxim avers that any rash action ultimately leads to ruin.

494. भल्लूकमुष्टिन्यायः

This maxim describes the firm grip of any person by giving an example of a bear whose hold is so firm that it becomes very difficult for any person to get release out of it.

495. भस्मच्छन्नाग्निन्यायः

The maxim informs that a bright man may seem to be

pale owing to some calamities. But he shines as usual, like fire afterward. The fire may seem to be silent when it is covered with ashes but once the ash is removed, it burns brightly again.

496. भस्त्रिकालवित्रन्यायः

If something is kept in a bellowing bag, nothing will happen to it even though air is taken in and puffed out. But if a sickle is kept, its movenent will simply tear off the billowing bag. A dectructive thing should not be kept near, the maxim advises.

497. भाण्डानुसारिस्नेहन्यायः

Ex. कः पुनरनुशयो नामेति। केचित्तावदाहुः। स्वर्गस्थस्य कर्मणो भुक्तफलस्यावशेषः कश्चिदनुशयो नाम भाण्डानुसारिस्नेहवत्। यथा हि स्नेहभाण्डं रिप्यमानं न सर्वात्मना रिच्यते भाण्डानुसार्येव कश्चित् स्नेहशेषोऽतिष्ठते, तथाऽनुशयोऽमीति।

–शाङ्करभाष्य, ब्रह्मसूत्र 3.1.8

The maxim says that a man living in some other world, may sojourn to different world. But he carries some remnants of the previous life in that world, as there will be some oil sticking to a vessel, even though oil is completely emptied from it.

498. भाण्डालेख्यन्यायः

Cf. **खण्डन खण्डखाद्य commentary, p. 289.**

The maxim tells that specialities of some pictures engraved on some metalware are those of the pictures only. The metal has nothing to do with them.

499. भामतीन्यायः

The maxim shows how the same name may have different effects on different persons, Bhāmati (is the name of a lady) may delight her husband, may cause anguish to her co-wife or may lure some other person by her beauty.

500. भावार्थाधिकरणन्यायः

Cf. **आपदेव, मीमांसान्यायप्रकाश, पृ० 851.**

In Mimāṁsā terminology, the verbal part of any Vedic injunction is called Bhāvanā, of which Ārthī is one of the two types—Kim Bhavayet, Kena Bhavayet, Katham Bhāvayet are the three basic questions. The third one gets the reply about the means or Karaṇa, according to Bhāvārthādhikaraṇa.

501. भिक्षुताडितश्वानन्यायः

This maxim alludes to the noble nature of a dog. Once a dog approached Rāma and complained that a beggar had beaten it severely. The king summoned the beggar who pleaded that the dog always followed him wherever he went. Because of the fear of the barking dog, no body came near him to give alms. So he bet it. The dog, in return pleaded that it was a worshipper in a temple, in its earlier birth. It used to eat the food prepared for the deity and Brāhmaṇas. He accepted the punishment and requested the king to appoint the beggar as a worshipper of the temple. Then the dog went to Kāśī and died there. It had the sacred Darśana of Sri Rāma and reached the ultimate goal—i.e. Mokṣa.

502. भिक्षुपादप्रसारण न्यायः

Ex. (1) भिक्षुपादप्रसरणन्यायेन क्षणभङ्गाद्यभिधामुखेन स्वामित्वानुकूल्यवेदनीयत्वानुगजत्वसर्वसत्यत्वाभ्रम व्यावर्तनेन सर्वशून्यतायामेव प्रसरणम्।

—सर्वदर्शनसङ्ग्रह, दर्शन, पृ० 14

(2) वेङ्कटनाथ, तत्त्वमुक्ताकलापः, पृ० 254

Once a beggar came to the house of a rich man, who allowed him to take rest in his house. The cunning beggar slowly tried to extend his legs and thus secured more space in that house. He went on soliciting more and more things from the rich man. The maxim shows that a shrewd man accepts a paltry offering at the beginning only to secure more and more gradually.

503. भिक्षुभिया स्थाल्यनधिश्रयणन्यायः

Simply because the beggars are likely to come, one does not stop cooking in a vessel. Similarly, says the maxim, one should decide the desirability or otherwise by independant ways and should not be affraid of minor obstacles.

504. भित्तिबिडालन्यायः

A cat, sitting on the parapit wall, seems to be quiet, but it can jump to the side which is advantageous to it. Thus, says the maxim that an ordinary man tends to the beneficial side, maintaining a close watch over the circumstances.

505. भिल्लीचन्दनन्यायः

Ex. अतिपरिचयादवज्ञा सन्ततगमनादनादरो भवति।
मलये भिल्लपुरन्ध्री चन्दनतरुकाष्ठमिन्धनं कुरुते॥
—शार्ङ्गधरपद्धति नीति, 83

There are many sandal-wood trees on the Malaya mountain. A large number of sandle trees grow there and an ample stock of this costly, fragrant wood can be collected on this mountain. The Bhil,tribal-ladies do not have any idea about the value of this wood. They collect the wood from the forest and burn it like fuel. The maxim underscores the fact-that Familiarity breeds contempt.

506. भीमभासदृढन्यायः

Ex. दामव्यालकटन्यायो न स्यात्तव कदाचन।
भीम भास दृढंन्यायः सर्वदा तेऽस्तु राघव।। –योगवासिष्ठ

This maxim refers to an episode in the Yogavāsisṭha. Sabara, a demon, possessing miraculous powers, created three demons called Bhīma, Bhāsa and Dṛdha. But later, they acquired the supreme knowledge in contrast with those three demons Dāma. Vyāla and Kaṭa who were reduced to reprehensible birth like that of a mosquito, due to their ignorance.

507. भूमिरधिकन्यायः

A soldier who is desirous of attaining skill in defeating the enemy troops, practises that art of fighting by drawing imaginery pictures on the ground and thinks of military strategy in a playway manner.

508. भूलिङ्गशकुनिन्यायः

Ex. न गाथा माथिनं शास्ति बहु चेदपि गायति।
प्रकृति यान्ति भूतानि भूलिङ्गगशकुनिर्यथा।

–महाभारत; सा० 340

The maxim tells that some men, though clever, are hypocrites in their behaviour. They do exactly opposite of what they say. Bhulinga bird is found in the Himalaya region. It always exorts the people not to do any rash, adventurous act and should remain away from venturous deed! But at the same time, it does an adventurous act of entering the jaw of a lion to pickup some flesh pieces, attached to its teeth.

509. भूशैत्योष्णन्यायः

Ex. उष्णत्वमग्न्यातपसंप्रयोगाच्छैत्यं हि यत्सा प्रकृतिर्जलस्य।

–रघुवंश, V. 54

Cf. जलौष्ण्यन्याय, वायुशैत्योष्ण्यन्याय.

The maxim is used to point out some external changes in objects, the common properties of which adopt peculiar external properties. Water is naturally cool but becomes hot when it contacts cold or heat, though temporarily.

510. भृङ्गकीटन्यायः

A bee picks out an insect from the sand. It flies around that insect with its fluttering sound and then converts that insect in a bee like insect. Similarly, a teacher also makes his student learned like himself by repeated efforts in giving him education.

511. भेर्याघातन्यायः

With the beating of a drum, one may walk ten steps, twenty steps, thirty steps or even forty steps, according to one's own stamina or onés own physical strength. The maxim says that one does the work according to one's capacity. There cannot be one rule for all.

512. भ्रमरन्यायः

When a bee goes near a thorny bush, it avoids the thorns and goes to the flowers only. So also, a good person accepts the good qualities and is indifferent to the bad qualities of others.

Moreover, a selfish person approaches only that person by whom he can be benefitted otherwise he shuns him, exactly in a manner in which a person approaches an affluent person and discards him when that chance is not there.

A bee can easily make a hole in any hard substance like wood but once it enters into the delicate, loving petals of the beautiful, colourful lotus, it cannot come out. —सा० 323, 324, 325

The maxim conveys the above three meanings.

513. भ्वादिन्यायः

प्रभाव, अनुभव, परिभव, सम्भव, विभव। —The prefixes change the meaning of the roots.

This maxim says that roots in grammar convey different meanings especially, when prefix (upasarga) is added to them. Similarly, one unique Brahman appears to be multifarious, owing to the adjuncts.

514. मक्षिकातन्तुनाभन्यायः

A spider exudes out its saliva like secretion and weaves a delicate net from the tiny threads out of its saliva. When a fly is caught in that net, the spider catches it and kills it. Similarly, says the maxim that a shrewd and wicked person also weaves a net of his cunning ways and traps the people by his wicked manner and destroys them in the end.

515. मक्षिकान्यायः

A fly sits on the wounded part without caring the entire body. So also, the wicked people take pleasure in finding faults of others without looking at their good point, says the maxim.

516. मज्जनोन्मज्जनन्यायः

Ex. अपारसंसारसमुद्रमध्ये निमज्जतो मे शरणं किमस्ति।
गुरो कृपालो कृपया वदेतद् विश्वेशपादाम्बुज दीर्घनौका॥

A novice in swimming, sometimes comes up from the water and sometimes goes down into the water. He has no control on his own present position. Similarly, the maxim remarks that a man sometimes rises up and sometimes goes down in this worldly ocean. He is saved or drowned in the ocean of worldly phenomenon depends till he gets the support of the Almighty.

517. **मञ्जूषाखुन्यायः**

Once a mouse entered the bag of a serpent charmer with a desire of getting something to eat. But there was a serpent, sitting in that bag. No sooner did the mouse enter the bag than the serpent swallowed it. The maxim warns that non-vigilance is dangerous.

518. **मणिप्रदीपप्रभान्यायः**

Ex. स्वयं भ्रमोऽपि संवादी यथा सम्यक्फलप्रदः।
ब्रह्मतत्त्वोपासनापि तथा मुक्तिफलप्रदा॥

A lamp was burning under a lid at one place in a temple giving rise to a circular shade. At another place, there was actually a jewel which created a bright halo. Seeing the round shades, two persons ran there shouting "jewel, jewel". The jewel cognition of both of them was false. One who ran there thinking that there was jewel, did not get it but he who ran considering the lustre of the jewel, ultimately got it. The illusion about the jewel, of the light of the lamp is disharmonious delusion while the delusion of a jewel on the light of the jewel is harmonious delusion.

—सा० 458

519. **मण्डूकतोलनन्यायः**

If frogs are kept on one pan of a balance for weighing them, no weight can be ascertained, as they jump out of the weighing pan or even jump inside the pan. The maxim describes an uncertain, chaotic situation.

520. मण्डूकप्लुतिन्यायः

The habit of a frog is to leap forward skipping over some intermediary thing. Wherever some intermediary steps are omitted, while jumping upto the further one, this maxim called the maxim of "the frogś leap" becomes applicable. For example in a group of four Sūtras of Paṇini, the first sūtra is not repeated in the second one, it jumps to the fourth one, leaving the middle two sūtras.

521. मण्डूकमक्षिकान्यायः

A frog which is caught in the mouth of a snake and is on the point of destruction, tries to catch a fly which comes in front of it. Thus the maxim shows that greed does not die even in front of death.

522. मत्तकाशिनीन्यायः

If a very beauliful lady (Mattakāsinī) to whom many paramours are easily available, displays her passion for birds and aninals, how astonishing it is! This maxim expresses that astonishment when one expresses one's satisfaction on lesser benefit when ample benefits are available.

—सा० 173

523. मत्स्यकण्टकन्यायः

यथा कश्चिन्मासार्थी मत्स्यान् सशकलान् सकण्टकानाहरति नान्तरीयकत्वात्। स यावदादेयं तावदादाय शकलकण्टकानुत्सृजति।

A fisherman catches a fish as a whole with its shells also. He removes the thorny parts from its body before eating. Similarly, the maxim implies that the adjuncts also are accepted to understand clearly the secondary meaning of Tattvamasi. Later on, it is changed by (resorting) to the secondary sense of partially renouncing it. (Bhāga tyāga lakṣaṇā).

524. मधुकरराजमधुमक्षिकान्यायः

Ex. इन्द्रियेभ्यः परंमनः।

—भगवद्गीता-III, 42

The maxim means that the sense organs of a person obey the mind (citta), like the bees obeying the orders of the king bee. All the sense organs of men are the followers of the mind only.

525. मधुररसभाविताम्रबीजन्यायः

If a mango tree is planted in a well-cultivated land whole-heartedly, the sweetness rises up right from the sprout, leaves, blossoms and lastly to the fruit itself. The maxim implies—Reap as you sow, sow as you reap.

526. मध्यममणिन्यायः

There are white or blue jewels in a necklace. Some five or seven jewels are woven on both the sides. The central jewel is taken into account (it is also counted) from whatever side the counting may commence. This maxim maintains that the person centrally situated (in an impartial position) is always an important one.

527. मरुमरीचिकान्यायः

नायमत्र प्रस्तावो मृगतृष्णिकेव विषादाय कल्पेत्।

—अभिज्ञान शाकुन्तल, 7

This is used to describe a delusion. If one stands in a desert, he sees some delusive appearance of flowing water. The maxim refers to a scene or event which appear (falsely) and is never seen in reality. This delusion is also called "delusion of a deer", as the thirsty deer in the desert are also deluded by the (false) scenes of flowing water.

528. मर्कटकिशोरन्यायः

The young ones of a female monkey cling fast to their mother. The mother may jump here and there but the young ones are safe because their embracing contact is very firm. Similarly, declares the maxim, the devotees cling to the deity. They are ardently devoted to the deity and thus always enjoy safety with the deity.

529. मर्कटमदिरान्यायः

A monkey is a very fickle animal. If it drinks liquor and then a scorpion bites it, its hectic, peculiar movements are only to be imagined! If a drunken man is possessed by a ghost or bitten by a scorpion, his plight cannot be imagined.

530. मर्कटानलतापशान्तिन्यायः

Ex. उपदेशो हि मूर्खाणां प्रकोपाय न शान्तये।

—पञ्चतन्त्र 1.420

Once on a cold day, some monkeys began to search for fire to warm up their bodies. They saw some red objects resembling fire sparks. They were actually Gunja fruits. The monkeys collected them and began to blow air to make them burn like fire. The sparrow which was observing their fruitless efforts tried to convince them by telling that the red objects were not fire sparks but Gunjā fruits only. The monkeys did not like this unnecessary interference of the sparrow. They became furious and killed it. The maxim tells that it is futile to convince an ignorant fool, even truth infuriates them. One should not advise the fool, as it may result in adverse reaction only.

531. मलिनदर्पणन्यायः

Ex. प्रायेणोत्तम मध्यमाधमगुणाः संसर्जतो जायते।

—भतृ नीतिशतक 58.

A mirror is originally clean but its clarity is obliterated by dust particles deposited on it. So also, maintains the maxim that a person is good normally and by nature but becomes bad in the company of the bad persons.

—सा० 100

532. मल्लग्रामन्यायः

Cf. **आम्रवणन्याय, ब्राह्मणग्रामन्यायः**

The maxim throws light on a common practice. Many people live in a town but if there are many wrestlers living in that place, the town is known as a wrestler-town (Mallagrāma). Nomenclatures are given by the large quantitative content.

533. महानसशशन्यायः

The rabbits kept in a kitchen, cannot go anywhere. The maxim states that people confined to a place, have no freedom of movement.

534. महामत्स्यतीरन्यायः

Ex. महामत्स्य उभे कूले सञ्चरति, पूर्वं चापरं चैव मेवायं पुरुष एतान् सञ्चरति स्वप्नान्तं बुद्धानां चेति।

—बृहदारण्यक उप. IV. 3.18; सा० 897

A big fish moves from one bank of the river to the other bank but it is not connected with the bank. The maxim says that the embodied soul experiences different states like wakefulness but it is not affected by them.

535. **महावातगजन्यायः**

A big hurricane can carry away heavy animal like an elephant with it; then what to say about light and weak animals or objects! The heavy storm can easily carry away light objects and weak and small animals or beings. The indeclinable 'Kimuta' is used in this case. Hence the name of the maxim—Kaimutika.

536. **मात्स्यन्यायः**

Ex. (1) दुर्बलं बलवन्तो हि मत्स्या मत्स्य विशेषतः।
भक्षयन्ति सदा वृत्तिर्विहिता नः सनातनी॥

—महाभारत 3.185.8

(2) राजा चेन्न भवेल्लोके पृथिव्यां दण्डधारकः।
जले मत्स्यानिवाभक्ष्यन् दुर्बलं बलवत्तराः॥
अराजकाः प्रजाः पूर्वं विनेशुरिति नः श्रुतम्।
परस्परं भक्षयन्तो मत्स्या इव जले कृशान्॥

—महाभारत 13.27, 16, 17

(3) (दण्डः) अप्रणीतो हि मात्स्यंन्यायमुद्भावयति।
बलीयानबलं हि ग्रसते दण्डधराभावे।

—कौटिल्य 1.4

A big fish swallows a small fish. Similarly a strong person always oppresses the weak person observes the present maxim.

537. **मारिषशाकदासन्यायः**

Once upon a time, a poor householder used to give leafy vegetable called Māriṣa (Rājagirā) to all those who used to approach him. After his death, he was born in a rich family. But the memory of his earlier life was intact. So he began to distribute the same leafy vegetables to the poor and needy. That was a very low type of charity. The maxim gives this instance and remarks that the merit acqired by small charity in the state of poverty cannot be aquired by doing the same charity in rich, prosperous life.

538. मार्जारकवलन्यायः

When many persons sit together for food, they put the morsels of food in their mouth by taking them in their hands. If a cat is observing this, it thinks that the persons are taking food in their hands with a view to give it to itself (i.e.cat). The maxim generalizes this incident by saying that selfish persons think that activities which others do are in their favour only.

539. मार्जारकिशोरन्यायः

Ex. अनन्याश्चिन्तयन्तो मां ये जनाः पर्युपासते।
तेषां नित्याभियुक्तानां योगक्षेमं वहाम्यहम्॥

—भगवद्गीता, 9.46

When a female cat carries its young ones from one place to another place, it holds them carefully in its mouth. The young ones have nothing to do because they are safe with the mother cat. This is in contrast with the practice of a female monkey where the youngone has to hold the mother tightly. The maxim, on the basis of this fact asserts that the God himself looks after the devotees.

540. मार्जारदुग्धपानन्यायः

When a cat drinks milk, it closes its eyes. It thinks that nobody is looking at it. Similarly. a person who commits some sinful acts also thinks that he can do them safely, as he is not seen by anybody, doing that sinful act (actully, God observes all his acts).

541. मार्जालाभ्यञ्जनन्यायः

If a cat is massaged with oil and is given hot water bath, it is of no use. All the efforts and the effect of bath are all invain. The maxim describes the efforts of a person which are fruitless.

542. माषराशिप्रविष्टमपीन्यायः

Ex. शकारः-भाव भाव, बलीयसि खल्वन्धकारे माषराशि, प्रविष्टेव मसीगुटिका दृश्यमानैव प्रनष्टा वसन्तसेना॥

–मृच्छकटिक, Act, I

The māṣa grain is black. Even if some collyrium is applied to the heap of this grain, that black colour will be easily absorbed by the māṣa grain. The maxim states that one colour can be easily absorbed or covered by some thing of the same colour and cannot be seen distinctly.

543. मीमांसान्यायः

The Mimāṁsā rules are technical in nature, but many of them can be utilized. They can describe certain events of worldly life. In this collection of worldly maxims, however, they are not taken to avoid prolixity. About eleven Miāṁsās are mentioned below.

होलिकाधिकरणन्याय, वाङ्नियमन्याय, दर्वीहोमन्याय, वाक्यार्थप्रति-पत्तिन्यायं, अङ्गुणनिषेधेतारदर्प्यादितिन्याय, पशुसोमार धीकरणन्याय, निषादस्थपतिन्यायं, प्रतिप्रदानं गुण आवर्तनीयं इतिन्याय, गुणविरोध न्याय।

Somemore Mīmāmsā maxims are enumerated, on pp. 1339 & 1354 in Vol.-V, Part-II, History of Dharmasāstra.

544. मुञ्जादिषीकोद्धरणन्यायः

Ex. (1) यथा मुञ्जादिषीकैवमात्मा युक्त्या समुद्धृतः।
शरीरत्रितयाद् धीरैः परब्रह्मैवे जायते॥

—पञ्चदशी, 1; तत्त्वविवेक, 42

(2) अङ्गुष्ठमात्रः पुरुषोऽन्तरात्मा सदा जनानां हृदये सन्निविष्टः। तं स्वाच्छरीरात्प्रवृहेन्मुञ्जदिवैषीकां धैर्येणं तं विद्याच्छुक्रममृतम्॥

—कठोपनिषद् 6.17

In the inner side of the Muñjā grass, there is a thread like long and soft grass, resembling a thin tube. That tube like grass can be carefully taken out from the Munjā grass. The maxim , referring to this speciality, tells that the persons observing celibacy, can slowly separate themselves from the three types of bodies. Then the self becomes one with the Brahman which is of the nature of consciousness or Bliss.

545. मुण्डितशिरोनक्षत्रान्वेषणन्यायः

Trying to find an auspicious time for the work already done is useless. The maxim says that it is as useless as the action of a man who first gets his head shaved and then tries to find out any auspicious time, day or moment for it.

546. मूषासिक्तताम्रन्यायः

Ex. मूषासिक्तं यथा ताम्रं तन्निमं जायते तथा।
रूपादीन् व्याप्नुपच्चित्तं तन्निमं दृश्यते, ध्रुवम्॥

—पञ्चदशी, द्वैतविवेक 4, 28

Hot liquid metal is poured in a crucible. That metal liquid takes some shape when it is cooled down. The maxim describes the process of mind indicating that the inner Citta (mind) permeates external forms. It makes them the object of perception and in the end takes the shape of the object of perception itself.

547. मूषिकविषाणन्यायः

The maxim is put to use at the time of describing the impossible things like the horns of the rat.

548. मूषिकसर्पपटिकान्यायः

Many things were kept in a box. A serpent also made its entry into it, thinking that it could get some food articles to eat; A rat made a hole to that box and entered it. Seeing the mouse, the snake tried to catch hold of it but the mouse easily escaped through the same hole made by it. Based on this event, the maxim remarks that a being may escape from sorrow to joy and vice a versa too.

549. मूलक्रिमिन्यायः

The maxim says that all those things which are spoiled or damaged at the beginning only, perish ulimately as the tree ultimately dies (dries up) when its roots are spoied by the insects.

550. मृगतृष्णान्यायः

Ex. रे चित्त चिन्तय चिरं चरणौ मुरारैः
पारं गमिष्यसि यत्तो भवसागरस्य।
पुत्रः कलत्रमितरे सुहृदः सहायाः
सर्वं विलोकय सखे मृगतृष्णिकामम्।

The maxim illustrates the phenomenon of delusion b[y] pointing how the deer try to run after imaginery wave[s] of water, to quench their thirst. Their delusion i[s] sometimes fatal to them-According to Vedānta, thi[s] world is also a kind of delusion. —सा० 44

551. मृद्घटन्यायः

मृद्घट दव सुरवमेद्यो दुःसधानश्च दुर्जनो भवति।
सुजनस्तु कनकघट इव दुर्भेदः सुकरसंधिश्च॥

—पंचतन्त्र, मित्रसम्प्राप्ति-38

An earthen jar can be fashioned in a short time but it can be broken or destroyed within a short time. A metal jar requires a good deal of time for perparation but it cannot be broken easily. It lasts for a long time. The maxim is applicable to a similar type of friendship. When it is formed quickly, perishes quickly. But the friendship which is made after a long time, lasts long and is never broken easily.

552. मेघचातकन्यायः

The maxim describes the real friendship as one which is there between the Cātaka bird and the cloud. The cātaka takes water from the clouds only and not from anywhere else.

553. मेषयुद्धन्यायः

Once two rams were fighting with each othet. A jackal intervened and tried to stop them from fighting but alas, it was killed in that confusion. This maxim suggests that when two persons of equal strength are fighting, and if a weak person intervenes in that fight, there is a danger of the loss of his own life.

554. यथाराज्ञन्यायः

People often try to imitate their king—his merits or demerits. So the maxim declares—As the king, so the subjects. The subjects of the empire follow the foot steps of their king only whether they imitate his virtues or his vices.

555. यथासङ्ख्यन्यायः

If there are equal number of subjects and predicates in a sentence, then they are connected in order of their placements i.e first subject with first predicate and so on. That is what this maxim implies by saying 'Yathā-samkhya'. For example, you conquer, entertain and endure—an enemy, a friend and the calamity respectively.

556. यदन्तरन्यायः

The maxim tells about the tendency of the people to consider or to relate the earlier event to the cause of the subsequent one, linking them by causal relation. When a newly wedded bride enters her in-law's house and some good fortune occurs, there it is related to the good fortune or good and auspicious entry of the bride.

557. यववराहन्यायः

Ex. यववराहन्यायःकरणन्यायेन लोकप्रसिद्धिः शास्त्रीयप्रद्धिया बाध्येत्याह।

—आननदगिरिटीका, ब्रह्मसूत्र, शांकरभाष्य II.3.45

The maxim speaks about different connotations of the same words in urban and rural languages, giving the example of Yava (barley) and Varāha (a boar).

558. यवागूगर्तप्लवनन्यायः

युक्ताहारविहारस्य युक्तचेष्टस्य कर्मसु।
युक्तस्वप्नावबोधस्य योगो भवति दुःखहः॥

—गीता, VI.17

Gruel (Yavāgū) in a particular quantity may give pleasure and satisfaction to a person. But how can he get the same joy if he swims in a ditch full of this gruel? The maxim indirectly advises the people to be satisfied with a limited quantity of whatever thing they desire.

559. **याचितकमण्डनन्यायः**

Ex.अस्याः मुखश्रीप्रतिबिम्बमेव जलाच्च तातान्मुकुराच्चमित्रान्।
अभ्यर्थ धत्तः खलु पद्मचन्द्रौ विभूषणं याचितकं कदाचित्॥
—श्रीहर्ष, नैषधीयचरित, 8.56

Some people who have no ornaments of their own, decorate their bodies with borrowed ornaments. This desire for parading oneself in the people, even without proper resources is vented out by the maxim.

560. **यावत्तैलंतावदाख्यानम्न्यायः**

The religious discourses can go on till there is oil in the lamp. Once it is exhausted, there was darkness and consequently no narration continue. The maxim, on the strength of this event tells that the work can be done so long as the means or resources are available.

561. **'यावद्वचनंवाचनिकम्' न्यायः**

Ex. (i) **कश्चात्र विशेषः। स यदि वाचनिकस्ततो यावद्वचनमेव कर्तव्यः।** —तन्त्रवार्तिक, V.3.12.

(ii) शाबर भाष्य, मीमांसासूत्र, V.4.11; V.3.12.

This maxim is applied to certain conditions in the Śāstra literature to those words or statements, in which the words are sufficient enough to express the meaning of the statement. No additional words or explanations are required.

562. **युध्यत्कुक्कुटन्यायः**

The maxim states that some men go on fighting with

foolhardiness, like the two cocks which continue to fight though they bleed profusely.

563. यूकाभियान्यानाश्रयणन्यायः

Ex. काव्यं शुभे विरचिते खलु नो खलेभ्यः
कश्चिद् गुणो भवति यद्यपि सम्प्रतीह।
कुर्यां तथापि सुजनार्थमिदं यतः किं
यूकाभयेन परिधान विमोक्षणं स्यात्।। —सुभाषितम्

Should one discard a blanket because the bed.bugs or lice in it are likely to bite? Should one not write poems because many uninterested and wicked people are unable to appreciate the poems? This maxim is applicable to a person who wants to give up the benefits, simply because some loss is likely to occur.

564. यूपपशुन्यायः

Once the animal is tied to the sacrificial post, its death becomes certain. Similarly, when the early signs are seen, the consequences begin to appear. This is the purport of the maxim.

565. रक्तपटन्यायः

When a sentence has no expectancy (for the import) and when no other word is necessary for the proper understanding of the sentence, some expectancy is deliberately created and a consistency of meaning is established. Though thereis—no expetancy in "There is no cloth." But expectancy can be created by the question "of what type"? is suggested by the word "red." There is a cloth can be expanded into there is a red cloth. The maxim incorporates this device.

—सा० 501

566. रज्जुसर्पन्यायः

This maxim is based on the false imposition of serpent

on a rope. This delusion changes due to false imposition called Vivarta. From the abstract Brahman, the multifarious world cannot take its rise. Then what is the phenomenon of the world? Actually, the world is only a false appearance, on the substratum of the Brahman, as there is the false appearance of the serpent on a rope. This example is often repeated in the works on Advaita philosophy.

567. रण्डाविवाहन्यायः

An unchaste woman thinking of marriage! Though astonishing, it should be accepted that an unchaste woman does have passionate feelings but even then, she cannot satisfy her passion with only one man with whom she is wedded. The maxim tells, that is why this woman does not think about marriage.

568. रथकाराधिकरणन्यायः

Ex. आधाने श्रूयते। वर्षासु रथकार आदधीतेति, चेत् नैवम्। सङ्कीर्णजातिविशेषे रूढत्वात्। वैश्यायां क्षत्रियादुत्पन्नो महिष्यः।

शूद्रायां वैश्यादुत्पन्नः करणी। तस्यां करण्यां माहिष्यादुत्पन्नो रथकारः।

तथां च याज्ञवल्क्यः। माहिष्येण करण्यां तु रथकारः प्रजायते। इति। —जैमिनीयन्यायमाला विस्तार

The word Rathakāra means a man fashioning a chariot, a carpenter. But he is not included among the first three Varṇas Thus the conventional meaning is stronger than the derivative meaning. This is what is conveyed by the maxim. A child of a Vaisya lady and a Śudra husband is 'Karaṇi' When a son is born from Karaṇi and a Māhiṣya husband, he is called a Rathakāra.

569. रथवडवान्यायः

The female horses yoked to a chariot, can draw the chariot well, if they make concerted effort. Similarly, suggests the maxim, if the chariot of worldly life is to be drawn safely, the two wheels in the form of the wife and husband should work smoothly and amicably.

—सा० 393

570. रथ्यादीपन्यायः

When a lamp is being carried on a high way, the light of the lamp falls on a place, then comes the actual lamp. The light moves forward and that place is darkened slightly. Thus a regular chasing game takes place between the light and the darkness on the highway. The maxim declares that the life is also a game of light and darkness i.e. joy and sorrow, which occur alternately in life.

571. रथ्याप्रवाहन्यायः

The water in the rainy season flows on the roads and then meets the streams or rivers. So also, asserts the maxim that the small groups of followers in the fields of either politics or philosophy or similar other parlances, become one with the bigger groups.

572. रश्मितृणादिन्यायः

If the sunlight falls on the grass, various colours in it are clearly visible. But if it falls on the Sūryakānta jewel, fire is produced. The maxim on the basis of the above example says that a man may show mercy for one but the same man has hatred for another.

573. राजपुत्रप्रवेशन्यायः

One has to enter the capital city of a king in a disciplined manner. One cannot enter the city as he likes. It is better then to be cautious and enter the capital in a queue. This maxim is applicable to the situation where there is harmonious situation and where there is proper causal relation.

574. राजपुत्रव्याधन्यायः

Once a prince was handed over to a hunter by his stepmother. The hunter brought him up like his own son. Once a relative of the prince came to him and revealed that he was actually a prince only. Thereafter, he began to behave like a prince and cultivated Kṣ atriya quality in him and after some days, he became a king. The maxim remarks that the individual soul forgets its real nature and thinks itself to be a limited self only. By and by, with the advice of the preceptor, it realizes its own real state of the Brahman.

575. राजसेवान्यायः

Ex. **सेवाधर्मः परमगहनो योगिनामप्यगम्यः।**

—भतृहरि, नीतिशतक, 47

Doing service to anybody is a difficult work. Moreover it is very difficult to serve a king. Inspite of his hard and sincere work, the servant is always blamed. The maxim emphasizes the fact that serving anybody is a very difficult work.

576. रात्रिसत्रन्यायः

Ex. (1) मीमांसासूत्र 4.3.17-19.

(2) **तथा सर्वपापप्रदाहोऽपि ब्रह्मलिङ्गप्रश्नोत्तराभ्यां प्राधान्येन प्रतिपिपादयिषित तयोपक्रान्तस्योपासनस्य फलाकाङ्क्षया रात्रिसत्रन्यायेनार्थनादिकफलपरिणामे**

कर्तव्ये प्रधानार्थवाद इवाङ्गार्थवादे श्रुतस्यापि फलस्य ग्रहणौचित्यात्।

—कल्पतरुपरिमल, ब्रह्मसूत्र 3.3.31.

According to one of the Mimāṁsā rules, where no fruit is mentioned pertaining to a particular rite, the fruit mentioned in the laudatory passage should be taken as the fruit of the ritual. But when there is no mention of any fruit, it is laid down that the heaven is the fruit, especially in one of the Vedic rituals.

577. राधावेधोपमान्यायः

Ex. सा चेयती भवेत्कस्य सामग्रीयं सुदुर्लभा।
राधावेधोपमानेन धर्मप्राप्तिः प्रकीर्तिता।

—उपमितप्रपञ्चकथा, पृ० 413, 420, 434

The word 'Rādhāvedha' in the maxim means aiming at the centre of a target or hitting the bull's eye. It also means the seat for taking the aim. Rādhābhedin is an adjective used for Arjuna.

578. रामठकरण्डन्यायः

Even if asafoetida (रामठ) is removed from a box, the fragrance of it remains behind for sometime. Similarly states the maxim, fragrance or any courtesy leaves its effect behind. So much so that its effect lingers on, even if the individual bearing it goes away.

579. रासभक्रन्दितन्यायः

The braying of an ass is at the top of its voice, at the beginning but gradually it diminishes and becomes weak. The maxim remarks that the affection and love shown by a wicked person grows on decreasing gradually and finishes at the end.

580. राहुशिरोन्यायः

Ex. (i) द्वावेज ग्रसते दिनेश्वरनिशाप्राणेश्वरौ भास्वरौ।
भ्रातः पर्वजि पश्य दानवपतिः शीर्षाव शेषाकृतिः॥

(ii) जातग्रहत्वेऽपि, असितत्त्वात् सूर्यादिग्रहवन्न दृश्यते गगने पर्वकालादन्यत्र ब्रह्मवाक्यादिति।

—लौकिकन्याय साहस्त्री, पृ० 159-163

The head of Rāhu conveys many meanings like serpent and a demon. When Rāhu started drinking nectar, Viṣṇu cut off his head by his Sudarśana discus. Rāhu is also mentioned in astrology many a time. On the whole, the word Rāhu stands for inauspicious being.

581. रूमाक्षिप्तकाष्ठन्यायः

Ex. यथा रूमाया लवणाकरेषु
मेरौ यथा वोज्ज्वलरुक्मभूमौ।
यज्जायते तन्मयमेव तत् स्यात्
यथा भवेद् वेदविदात्मतुष्टिः॥ —तन्त्रवार्तिक, पृ० 132

बहूनामेकत्र परिणामो दृष्टः। तद्यथा। गवाश्वमहिषमातङ्गाना रूमान्तिक्षिप्तानामेको लवणत्वजातीयलक्षणः परिणामो वर्तितैलानलानां च प्रदीप इति।

—वाचस्पतिमिश्र, तत्त्ववैशारदी, योगसूत्र टीका 4-14

It is believed that when a piece of wood is thrown in the saline ocean called Rumā, it also becomes saltish. The maxim observing that effect, says that thing is converted into another thing merely remaining in its company. The nature of a thing changes if it comes in contact with another thing.

582. रूपसामान्यन्यायः

When two things have the same form or appearance, it

does not mean that the two things are completely identical. The rice brought in two houses is rice only but the name, colour, form, smell and in many other ways it is not the same—says this maxim.

583. रेखागवयन्यायः

Cf. (i) वाचस्पति मिश्र तात्पर्य टीका, पृ० 457.
(ii) वेदान्तकल्पतरु, पृ० 363

Once a villager asked a person the meaning of the word Gavaya (a wild bull). The man made a sketch of the animal with the help of some lines. The villager got some idea after seeing the picture. When he went to the forest, he saw a peculiar type of bull, resembling the picture drawn by that man. He could identify it to be a Gavaya. The maxim based on this incident says that a man gets some vague idea about the Ātmā. But with the help of a teacher, he gets a clear, distinct idea about the self.

584. रोगिरोगन्यायः

When a diseased person dies the disease from which he was suffering, also goes away with him. The maxim states that when an object (Dharmi) perishes, its property (Dharma) also perishes with the object automatically.

585. लतावृक्षन्यायः

Nobody can sustain without any support. This truth is exemplified in this maxim, taking an example of a creeper, which cannot grow independently. It has to take support of a tree.

586. लपोरशङ्खन्यायः

Ex. शङ्खिनी काञ्चनं दद्योदहं शङ्खो लपोरकः वादामि बहवाक्यानि न ददामि कपर्दिकाम्॥

The maxim maintains that a goddess called "Śankhinī" may offer gold to the devotee if she is pleased with him. But conch "Śankha" which simply produces sound (Laporaka) does not give anything. Just by similarity in name, one should not expect even a cowrie from the Śankha (the conch). —सा० 938

587. लवणामलकीन्यायः

The maxim speaks about unexpected meeting of persons which is like the coming together of an Āmalakī fruit from the forest and salt from the sea. Though the original taste of these two is different, the combined taste is very sweet.

588. लशुनभक्षणन्यायः

Garlic has a strong, lingering smell, so it is considered unholy and prohibited in the Śāstras. It has medicinal value also. One patient with an intention of curing his disease, ate it. But to his bad fate, his disease was not cured. He committed a sin by eating that prohibited thing. So he suffered from double disadvantage by eating garlic. The maxim aims at describing an act of double disadvantage by giving the example of garlic.

589. लाक्षारसावसिक्तकार्पासबीजन्यायः.

Ex. यस्मिन्नेव सन्ताने ह्याहिता कर्मवासना।
फलं तत्रैव बध्नाति कार्पासे रक्तता यथ।

—सर्पदर्शनसङ्ग्रह, आर्हतदर्शन; सा० 700

If cotton seeds are sprinkled over with the lac dye and then sown in the ground, the cotton yield which grows in the field in due course of time is also red cotton. Taking this example of the red cotton yield, the maxim says implicitly that the actions in this birth are tinged with the subliminal impressions.

590 लाङ्गलजीवनन्यायः

Ex. यथोक्तविद्याबोधित्वाद न्योऽपि तदभेदतः।
भवेदुपनिषन्नाम्ना लाङ्गलं जीवनं यथा।

—सुरेश्वराचार्य, सम्बन्धवार्तिक, पृ० 9

A plough is the invariable, inseparable means of livelihood for a farmer. The maxim, indicating this sense of inseparability becomes applicable when the means—end, cause—effect are said to be inseparable.

591. लाङ्गूलतरणन्यायः

The maxim speaks about the dangerous futile efforts. That effort is like trying to cross the river by catching the tail of a dog.

592. लूतातन्तुन्यायः

This maxim implies two senses—

(1) Just as a spider weaves a net from the threads, taken from its own body, the God also creates the phenomena of the world from his body only.

(2) As the spider is the instrumental and material cause of the threaded web, God is also the instrumental and material cause of the world.

—सा० 502

593. लोष्टप्रस्तरन्यायः

A stone and a clod of earth look alike but there is a lot of difference in their weight. The maxim states that the two things which apparently look alike, are quite different in their shape, weight and quality. —सा० 675

594. लोष्टलगुडन्यायः

The maxim gives the example of a stick and a clod of

earth. The stick completely destroys the clod of earth and converts the clod into the powder like substance. This implies that the stick and the clod of earth have a destroyer and the destroyed relation between these two. Whenever, this relation of a destroyer-destroyed is to be described, this maxim is applied. —सा॰ 503

595. लोहकपालन्यायः

The maxim compares the good and noble men with strong, sturdy iron. Iron does not stick to any other metal quickly nor does it grasp anything suddenly. Similarly, the good men also are very sturdy and so they do not bend quickly like iron.

596. लोहचुम्बकन्यायः

The maxim mentions an important charateristic of a magnet. Without moving from its place, without doing anything, sitting in one place only, the magnet converts an iron piece into a magnet by attracting the iron piece towards itself. This principle is applicable to the Sāṁkhya doctrine that Puruṣa attracts Prakṛti towards himself and makes her active. The activity of iron is attributed to magnet only.

597. लोहाग्निन्यायः

Iron acts like a fireball when it comes in contact with fire. The maxim infers that good or bad characteristics of a person arise only in a particular good or bad company of the people or friends.

598. वज्रलेपन्यायः

Vajra is the weapon of Indra or it also means a diamond. When two things are brought together, they stick to each other so firmly that it becomes difficult to separate them. This inseparable relation or condition between the two things is termed as Vajralepa. The weapon of Indra and the diamond also are unbreakable. Similarly the relation which cannot be broken or which cannot be erased or separated is described by this maxim.

599. वटबीजन्यायः

Ex. तं होवाच यं वै सोम्यैत्तमणिमानं न निभालयस एतस्य वै सौम्येषोऽणिम्न एव महान् न्यग्रोधस्तिष्ठति श्रद्धत्स्वं सोम्येति। स य एषोणिमैतदात्म्यामिदं सर्वं तत् सत्यं स आत्मा तत्त्वमसि श्वेतकेतो इति।

—छान्दोग्योपनिषद् 6.12.2.3

The maxim refers to the fact that from a small, tiny banyan seed, a big gigantic banyan tree evolves. Similarly from the most subtle Brahman, a big universe evolves.

600. वटेयक्षन्यायः

Cf. गतानुगतिको लोको न लोकः पारमार्थिकः। —सा० 25

There is a common blind belief that the Yakṣa or a particular power resides in a banyan tree. The people believe in it uncritically and so no one goes near that banyan tree without finding the reality ābout it. The maxim refers to such uncritical, undescerning belief.

601. वत्सक्षीरन्यायः

Ex. वत्सविवृद्धिनिमित्तं क्षीरस्य यथा प्रवृत्तिरज्ञस्य।
पुरुषविमोक्षनिमित्तं तथा प्रकृतिः प्रधान

—साङ्ख्यकारिका 58

An inert Prakṛti can bring about the liberation of Puruṣa. The maxim proves this by giving the example of milk which though insentient, brings about the nourishment in a calf.

602. वदतोव्याघातन्यायः

The maxim describes a situation in which the speaker utters something which contradicts his own words.

—सा० 693

603. वधूमाषमापनन्यायः

Example—

न चानवस्था अवश्यवेद्यत्वानभ्युपगमान्निश्चयवदन्यथा तु अनिश्चितनिश्चयस्य नाद्यनिश्चयोऽपि सिध्येत न चास्तवात्मन्यनिश्चय इति तादिदं वधूमाषमापन वृतानामनुहरति।

—आत्मविवेक, पृ० 87

This maxim tells that even good intentional actions also lead to undesirable situations. A Brāhmaṇa used to give a handful of blackgram to his wife to offer them to the beggars. When his son got married, he entrusted this work of distribution of alms to his daughter-in-law, thinking that less blackgrams will be carried in her little fists. This girl was very beautiful and good looking. So many beggars started coming to his house, not for blackgram but to have a look at this sweet lady, resulting in the distribution of a large quantity of blackgrams.

604. वध्यघातुकन्यायः

Example—

प्रतिपद्य पदार्थं हि विरोधात् तद्विरोधिनः।
पश्चादभावं जानाति वध्यधातुकवत् पदात्॥

—तैत्तिरीयवार्तिक, 2.1.65; सा० 380

The killer and the one going to be killed can never remain together. To indicate that hostile persons cannot stay together this maxim is employed.

605. वनव्याघ्रन्यायः

Ex. सोऽयं वनसिंहह्लदनक्रन्यायः। किरातै र्हन्तुं शक्योऽपि सिंहो महद्वनं शरणं प्रविश्य दुराधर्षस्तेभ्यो न विभेति वनं च तत्सिंहाधिष्ठानानुगृहीतं तैर्दुष्प्रवेशं भवति।

—वेदान्तकल्पतरुमल, पृ० 100

न स्याद् वनमृते व्याघ्राद् न स्यु र्व्याघ्रा ऋते वनम्।
वनं हि रक्ष्यते व्याघ्रैर्व्याघ्रान् रक्षति काननम्।।

—महाभारत, उद्योगपर्व 37-42; सा० 391

This maxim shows the mutually helping attitude of the tiger and the forest. The tiger protects the forest from encroachment and the forest gives shelter to the tiger.

606. वन्ध्यापुत्रन्यायः

This maxim can be applied to some improbable concepts like the son of a barren woman.

607. वम्रीकीटन्यायः

Ex. स्वच्छकन्दुकवम्रीकन्यायेनानिशमत्र ते।
भ्रमन्तो नाप्नुवन्त्यमन्यत्वं संविदन्ति च।।
व्योमस्य कन्दुकभ्रान्तपिपीलिकवटाकुलम्।
अद्यापि संस्थिता राजन्न च खेदं भजन्ति ते।।

—योगवासिष्ठ, निर्वाणप्रकरण (उत्तरार्ध) 131, 15-16

The maxim refers to a ball, revolving round and round. If some ants or small insects happen to climb on the ball, they also go on revolving. When revolving round and round continuously is to be described, this maxim is used.

608. वरगोष्ठीन्यायः

The relatives of the bridegroom and the relatives of the

bride come together and decide about the marriage of the bride and the bridegroom. If the relatives of both of them give their consent, then only the marriage takes place, says the maxim. 'Goṣṭhi' is a place where talks on certain topics are delivered. Secondarily, it means any place where discussions take place. This maxim refers to a place of discussion where some discussion about the selection of a bridegroom takes place. It may also mean a place where some decisions are taken after discussion of both the parties.

609. वरघातककन्यावरणन्यायः

The maxim literally means that the selection of a bride which may result in the peril of the bridegroom, should be avoided. By extended application it exhorts people not to undertake even desirable things if they are detrimental to the existence of some good-things.

610. वर्चोन्यायः

Cf. मीमांसासूत्र 3.8; 25-27

The maxim refers to a Mīmāṁsā rule that when lustre is solicited from the God of fire, the lustre is accrued by the sacrificer and not by the priest who actually articulates the request.

611. वलीमुखनारिकेलन्यायः

The monkey knows how to pluck the coconut fruit and make it fall down. It does not know how to use that fruit. The maxim describes an ignorant man who cannot make use of the available things.

612. वह्निधूमन्यायः

The maxim refers to the association of fire with the smoke. In inferences, the probans (Vyāpti) like--where there is smoke there is fire-plays an important role. The maxim refers to this probans only.

613. वह्निन्यायः

This maxim gives two special features of the fire:—

(i) Fire, though alone, can burn houses.

(ii) Many fire-particles (fire-sparks) emanate from the fire.

614. वह्निविस्फुलिङ्गन्यायः

The maxim suggests that from one Brahman only, many worldly things are produced, as many sparks are emitted from one fire only.

615. वाक्यभेदन्यायः

The maxim refers to a general rule of grammar that one sentence should convery one meaning only. But if the expressive ideas are more than one, then those fragments of that sentence are mutually dependent.

According to Mimāṁsā also, extracting many connotations from a sentence leads to a fault of 'split sentence' Mimāṁsā rules that if there is some injunction in one part, other parts of that sentence should be understood to be a laudatory passage to avoid Vākyabheda. If it is laid down that the inquiry into Dharma should be undertaken after the study of the Vedas, it does not mean that inquiry into Dharma is prohibited before Vedic studies; othewise the interpretation will lead to Vākyabhedha.

616. वाजिमन्दुरान्यायः

Mandurā means a stable, the place where horses are kept. The word Vājin means a horse. The word Vāji in this compound is redundant. There are many maxims where the word understood is repeated with or without any purpose.

617. वातप्रदीपन्यायः

The wind extinguishes a lamp. This act takes place in two ways.

(i) The thing perishes due to hostile causes.

(ii) Due to some reasons, the constituent parts of that thing get exhausted, The maxim is applicable to those cases.

618. वायुभक्षणन्यायः

'Eating of air' can also be taken as an activity connected with eating. The maxim prohibits other types of eating.

619. वायुशैत्यौष्ण्यन्यायः

Cf. भूशैत्यौष्णन्यायः, जलौष्ण्यन्यायः

Air becomes hot or cold owing to the presence or absence of heat or due to the contact or detachment with heat. They are, however not natural characteristics. The maxim is applicable to a case where an external or uncommon characteristic is superimposed externally.

620. वालिसुग्रीवन्यायः

The maxim is based on a common belief that Rāma killed Vāli who was the brother of Sugrīva. Nevertheless, Sugrīva is supposed to be stronger than Vāli.

621. वालुकान्यायः

This maxim is applied to a deluding phantasm like the one observed by a traveller in the desert. He sees flowing water from a distance but actually there is nothing but hot sand only.

622. विक्रीतगवीन्यायः

Ex. विक्रीय पण्यं मूल्येन क्रेतुः यन्न प्रदीयते।
विक्रीयासम्प्रदानं तद्विवादपदमुच्यते॥

The maxim echoes a situation where the owner of a thing retains its ownership, even after selling it away, as the owner of a cow wants to retain its ownership with him even after selling it, with some ulterior intention.

623. विक्रीते करिणि किमङ्कुशो विवाद न्यायः

Ex. i) सौमित्रिर्वदति विभीषणाय लङ्कां देहि त्वं
भुवनयते विनैव कोशम्।
सौमित्रिं प्रति निजगाद रामचन्द्रो
विक्रीते करिणि किमङ्कुशे विवादः॥

ii) नारब्धं कुचपरिरम्भणेषु वाम्यं
वैमत्यं विरचयति चुम्बने कदापि।
किं नीवीगतमबले रुणत्सि पाणिं
विक्रीते करिणि किमङ्कुशे विवादः॥ —सा० 750

The maxim decries the act of quarrelling for the price of a goud when the elephant is sold away. Quarrelling for petty things is futile and also foolish when the big thing is disposed off.

624. विनिगमनाविरहन्यायः

'Vinigamana' means considering only one aspect of some matters when other aspects are also possible. In astronomy some scholars concentrate on 'Dṛggaṇitā' method for the Sūryasiddhānta. But it cannot be proper to ascertian that Sūryasiddhānt doctrine is the only right one.

625. विषकुम्भपयोमुखन्यायः

Ex. परोक्षे कार्यहन्तारं प्रत्यक्षे प्रियवादिनम्।
वर्जयेत्तादृशं मित्रं विषकुम्भ पयोमुखम्॥

–हितोपदेश, मित्रलाभ, 74

This maxim describes a double tongued hypocrite who speaks sweet words but entertains poisonous attitude towards some person. He is, as the maxim says, like a jar full of poison but the mouth of the jar is filled with milk. Superficial innocence indeed!

626. विषकृमिन्यायः

Ex. विप्रास्मिन्नगरे महान् कथय कस्तालद्रुमाणां गणः
को दाता रजको ददाति वसनं प्रातर्गृहीत्वा निशि।
को दक्षः परदारवित्तहरणे सर्वोऽपि दक्षो जनः
कस्माज्जीवसि हे सखे विषकृमिन्यायेन जीवाम्यहम्।

–वृद्धचाणक्य

Certain type of environnent or atmosphere is harmful or unsuitable for many people but one who is born and brought up in that unhealthy atmosphere, can put up with that environment owing to his breeding and development in it, like the insect which is born in poison only, can endure poison, owing to its long stay or contact in poison.

627. विषवृक्षन्यायः

Ex. विषवृक्षोऽपि संवर्ध्य स्वयं च्छेत्तुमसाम्प्रतम्।

–कुमारसंभव II.55

हा हा मयेदं नो चारुकृतं यत्सुतभर्त्सनम्।
विषवृक्षोऽपि संवर्ध्य स्वयं च्छेत्तुमसाम्प्रतम्॥

If some work, though despicable, is accomplished with one's own endeavour, it is not proper to set it aside. It is not proper, declares the maxim, to uproot a tree, nurtured by oneself, even though it is poisonous.

628. विहङ्गमन्यायः

A bird can easily obtain a fruit which is high on the tree, unlike an ant or a monkey which cannot reach the sweet fruits which are on the top of the tree. Similarly, a person of the best qualification who has acquired right knowledge and has pure heart, can attain perfect knowledge as compared to other persons.

—सा० 517

629. वीचितरङ्गन्यायः

Ex. वीचीतरङ्गन्यायेन तदुत्पत्तिस्तु कीर्तिता।

'Vīci' means a billow. When many billows come together, they develop into a Taranga (a wave). Due to wind, a billow develops into the shape of a wave. The maxim emphasizes the slowly developing billow into a wave. This is how the sound waves also develop and spread.

—सा० 228

630. वृकबन्धनन्यायः

This maxim hints at doing a difficult thing by a simple device. If a wolf is to be caught, some butter is kept on the head of the wolf. As it melts, it enters the eyes of the wolf and thus it becomes easy to catch the wolf.

—सा० 251

631. वृक्षपक्षिन्यायः

The birds live on the trees. They build their nests on the tree and nourish their eggs on the trees only. Simply because they grow and fly on high trees, they cannot be superior to those which live on the lower earth. The eminence is judged by quality and not by the height of their birth places. —सा० 52

632. वृक्षप्रकम्पनन्यायः

The maxim tells as to how one can please all the people by one action only and gives the example of a man who had climbed on the tree. The people who were standing below, requested him to shake a particular branch of their choice. But the clever man shook the whole tree. By this simple act, he could shake almost all the branches and please every one. —सा० 52

633. वृक्षमूलनिषिञ्चनन्यायः

यथा तरोर्मूलनिषिञ्चनेन तृप्यन्ति तत्स्कन्धभुजोऽपि शाखाः।
प्राणोपहाराच्च यथेन्द्रियाणां तथैव सर्वार्हणमच्युतेज्याः॥

The maxim tells that by satisfying the vital breath, all the senses can be gratified as by pouring water at the root of a tree, it is (indirectly) supplied to all the branches of the tree. Similarly everyone will give respect if only. Hari is worshipped. (or if only one God Hari is worshipped, all the Gods will be satisfied).

634. वृद्धकुमारीवरन्यायः

Once Indra was pleased with an old virgin lady and gave her a boon. She asked from one boon many things very cleverly. She solicited that her sons should eat rice mixed with abundent ghee and milk in a plate made of Kāmsya metal. This clever lady asked for a husband, sons, cows, abundent grain and costly vessels etc. from one boon only. —सा० 2

635. वृद्धतरुणीन्यायः

The maxim asserts that if a young lady is married to

an old man, she would definitely pretent to be loyal to her husband.

636. वृद्धब्राह्मणवरन्याय

Once a blind, old, unmarried and poverty stricken man practised penance. The God was pleased by his sever penance and told him to ask for a boon. He uttered a small sentence but accomplished many things by that boon. His clever request was to see his grandson sitting on the throne. God was pleased by his clever request and granted wealth, health, progeny, wife and eyes also. —सा० 3

637. वृद्धवेश्यान्यायः

When a courtesan becomes old, she pretends to be penelope. The maxim based on this fact, implies that a person thinks himself to be pious, simple and non-violent when he becomes old and weak. This attitude is developed owing to helplessness and not by virtue.

638. वृश्चिकचोरन्यायः

A thief was bitten by a scorpion. He began to cry loudly. He could not run away because of the pain. Hearing his loud cries, the people of the house gathered there. They saw the stolen articles and caught him red handed. The people also bet him severely. He could not do anything because of the unbearable pain. —The maxim speaks about this thief.

639. वृश्चिकवानरन्यायः

If a scorpion bites a monkey, its hectic movements go on increasing. It becomes more confused and begins to run here and there, out of pain. Monkey is a very unsteady animal. Because of the scorpion bite, it runs more excitedly out of pain. The maxim conveys that a fickle man becomes more and more confused, if he suffers from some pain.

640. वृश्चिकविदूषकन्यायः

A jester or a joker is always given a role of dancing and gambling. When he dances and makes fun, people and children laugh loudly to their heartś content. His funny ways and his artificial behaviour are a part of his acting. But if a scorpion bites him and out of sever pain, he begins to dance, people take it as fun only and no one will take it very seriously.

641. वेण्याकाशन्यायः

The two rivers, Gaṅgā and Yamunā flow separately but when they come together at Prayāga they become one and only one stream flows. Whether separate or united they get the same reflection of the sky. The maxim intends to show that there is no difference between Brahmā, Viṣṇu and Śiva. —सा० 127

642. वेतसन्यासन्यायः

When the rivers are in floods , many objects on the bank are washed away. But the reed grass (or cane) on the bank of the rivers, just bends down and then again raises its head when the floods are over. The maxim implies that the self-respected persons may bend. That means they may carry a low profile in the advetsity but they regain their normal form when the bad days or the calamity is over.

643. वेश्याकान्तन्यायः

The maxim alludes to the unsteady love of a courtesan. As she entertains many lovers, she cannot be loyal to any one of them.

644. वेश्यापुत्रजनकन्यायः

This maxim is used to describe a queer relation like that of a courtesan and her son, as she maintains relations with many people, it is difficult to ascertain the father of her son.

645. व्यपगतलेपालाबून्यायः

The maxim is based on a peculiar nature of a pumpkin. When the earth is applied to it, it goes down and sinks. When that applied clay is washed off, it starts floating on the water. The maxim implies the Jain doctrine that when a person is freed from action, he moves up and up. In this example the pumpkin is like an individual and the cover of earth is his Karman. —सा० 704

646. व्यपदेशिन्यायः

If a man has got only one son, he is the eldest and is also the youngest. When two characteristics are applicable to one only this maxim becomes applicable. By Vyapadeśa two qualities are superimposed on one object). —सा० 32

647. व्यभिचारिणीन्यायः

यथा व्यसनिनी नारी व्यग्रापि गृहकर्मणि।
तदेवास्वादयत्यन्तः परसङ्गरसायनम्॥
एवं तत्त्वे पदे शुद्धे धीरो विश्रान्तिमागतः।
तदेवास्वादयन्तर्बहिर्व्यवहरन्नपि॥

—लौकिकन्याय साहस्री; सा० 45

An unchaste lady always remembers the pleasant moments of contact which she had with the paramour, even though she is apparently busy in daily routine work. The maxim states the similar kind of joy of remembering is also felt by an aspirant who thinks of the exquisite joy of meditation over the Brahman.

648. व्याघ्रचोरधनुर्न्यायः

Some cunning fellows bend low before the people. But it shows their hypocritic nature. It is not their behaviour to bend before anybody. It is just the beginning of their nefarious activities. The maxim gives the example of a tiger, a thief and a bow whose bending augurs dangerous results. —सा० 809

649. व्याघ्रीक्षीरन्यायः

The maxim says that the milk of the tigress (or a lioness) becomes more effective when it is stored in a golden vessel. Similarly, advice imparted to the students who are endowed with good qualities like physical and mental control, becomes very effective and powerful when it is given by the teacher.

650. व्यालनकुलन्यायः

The maxim speaks of eternal enmity like the one between the snake and the mungoose.

651. व्रात्यसंस्कारन्यायः

Vrātya is one who has not undergone any Śaṁskara like Upanayana. Such a Brāhmaṇa is not qualified to solemnize Saṁskāras in others.

652. व्रीहिबीजन्यायः

When the seeds are sown, only the upper cover is the begining; gradually the inner milklike substance gets solidified and the grain is formed. That darkness (Tamas is manifested in Śiva; slowly comes activity (Rajas) and serenity (sattva)' the three Guṇas also personify Brahmā, Viṣṇu and Śiva.

653. शकुनिग्राहकगतिन्यायः

The maxim refers to the knave method of a fowler. The fowler quietly goes near the birds and cleverly catches the birds in a net.

654. शकुनिसूत्रन्यायः

Ex. यथा पक्षी च सूत्रं च नानावृक्षरसा यथा।
यथा नद्यः समुद्राश्च शुद्धोदलवणे यथा॥
चोरापहार्यौ च यथा पुंविषयावपि।
तथा जीवेश्वरौ भिन्नौ सर्वदैव विलक्षणौ॥

—लौकिकन्याय साहस्त्री; सा० 817

The maxim refers indirectly to the view of the dualists who believe that the individual self and the God are different though they are related to each other; as a bird and a chord are different, though the bird is tied with a string.

655. शङ्कूत्खातदंष्ट्रोरगन्यायः

The maxim remarks that a serpent whose fangs are removed becomes harmless. Even if it bites there is no venum in it. So it becomes non-poisonous and thus harmless. Similarly an enemy whose helpers are perished or are destroyed, cannot do anything. He becomes harmless. —सा० 288

656. शङ्खवेलान्यायः

The maxim underlines the importance of a particular relevance. A conch should be blown at a proper time, Coversely, when a conch is blown, the particular hour or time is indicated.

657. शतपत्रपत्रभेदनन्यायः

Cf. शतपत्रशतन्यायः, शतपत्रशातनन्यायः अत्रव्यङ्ग्यप्रतीते-

विभाषादि प्रतीतिकारणकत्पात् प्रकमोऽवश्यमस्ति। किन्तुपल-पत्रशत व्यतिभेदवल्लधवान् न संलक्ष्यते।

—साहित्यदर्पण

२. **यत्प्रदीपत्रप्रभाद्युक्तं सूक्ष्मकालोऽस्ति तत्र नः।**
दुर्लक्षस्तु यथा वेधः पद्मपत्रशते यथा॥

—श्लोकवार्तिक, 137.

The maxim speaks about a particular delusion.

That event takes place simultaneously sometime when a sharp needle is pierced through the hundred petals of a lotus flower. Their softness creates a delusion that all the hundred petals are pierced simutaneously, the needle has to loose the contact with the earlier one and then contact the next one. But this takes place so quickly, that a delusion is created that the needle has pierced the petals at the same time.

658. शते पञ्चाशदितिन्यायः

It is needless to say that the number fifty is included in the number hundred. The higher one includes the lower one of the same type. Sacrifice, charity are included in one comprehensive term merit. —सा० 489

659. शब्दसुखाश्रितकुरङ्गगतिन्यायः

The maxim tells that a deer which is very much enticed by music can be easily caught by playing music near it. This means that one can be easily deceived by one's habit only.

660. शरपुरुषीयन्यायः

Cf. अजाकृपाणीयन्यायः, खल्वाटविल्वीयन्यायः.

Once a perosn was taking an aim to shoot an arrow at a particular target. The arrow hit a person who was passing in the range of the arrow and was killed. The maxim is applicable to such sudden, unexpected accidents.

661. शर्करोन्मज्जनीयन्यायः

Cf. शरपुरुषीयन्यायः

The maxim refers to an incident. It shows how a person who comes within the range, is affected by the action. A person was sprinkling sugar at one place. At that time a person just went across. As the action was continuous, the person who passed by was also sprinkled over and became smeared with sugar.

662. शलभन्यायः

A type of moth jumps on a lamp or on the flame of the lamp and is thus reduced to ashes instantly. The maxim is applicable to a person of the nature of a moth who brings about his own destruction thoughtlessly by rash action.

663. शल्यकवानाखुन्यायः

This maxim is generally used to convey the idea that a king should collect taxes from his subject very carefully. He should exploit the people very delicately like a mouse which takes out the lower portion of a man very slowly and cleverly.

664. शवोद्वर्तनन्यायः

There is no use of applying fragrant unguents to a corpse. Even if we apply, what is the use of it? The maxim decries useless actions like this.

665. शशविषाणन्यायः

Cf. वन्ध्यापुत्रन्यायः

The maxim is used to point out impossible and

improbable things like the horns of a hare. The rabbit does not have horns. It is only figment of imagination that we think of this kind of impossible things.

666. शाखाचङ्क्रमणन्यायः

Jumping from one branch to the other branch of a tree like the monkeys. The maxim is applicable to those persons who jump from one topic to another, without treating one topic thoroughly.

667. शाखाचन्द्रन्यायः

Ex. तरुशाखाग्रदृष्ट्यैव सोमं यद्वत् प्रदर्शयेत्।
निष्कोशं कोशदृष्ट्यैव प्रचीति ब्रह्म दृश्यते॥

—तैत्तिरीय भाष्य वार्तिक 2.1.232; सा० 249

The maxim applies to the action of a man. He wants to show the moon of the second day of the bright half of the month. But he points out to some other constellation, seen through the branches of a tree. The moon is hidden behind the branches. Slowly he tries to divert the attention to the moon.

668. शिखाकर्पूरन्यायः

When camphor is burnt over the flame of a lamp, the lamp may continue to burn for sometime but it extinguishes soon and even the camphor extinguishes with it. This example is adopted by this maxim which is used when the thing and its substratum both perish at the same time.

669. शिरोवेष्टनेन नासिकास्पर्शन्यायः

Cf. द्राविड प्राणायामन्यायः शिरोवेष्टनेनाङ्गुल्या नासिका प्रवेशवत्। —विज्ञानभिक्षु, ब्रह्मसूत्र टीका, 3.3.7

This is another version of Drāviḍa pranayama. If a

man is asked to show the tip of his nose, he will take his hand round his neck and then shows his nose. This shows the unnecessary cumbersome way of doing things. When a work can be done in the most easy method but unnecessarily uneasy or difficult method is adopted, this maxim is applicable.

670. शिलाक्षरन्यायः

The letters inscribed on a stone do not get blurred. They remain on the stone for a long time. Rather they remain there permanently. The maxim is applicable to such imperishable thing.

671. शीतकिरणकरावलम्बनन्यायः

To try to grab the rays of the moon by the hand is nothing but an impossible work. This maxim is applied to a situation where some work is being done which is beyond one's capacity. —सा० 889

672. शीतलाप्रस्तरन्यायः

A stone can be put to many uses. Even a sacred idol can be fashioned out of a stone. So it is clear that worthiness or worthlessness of an object, depends mostly on the sentimental attachment we have for it than on the substance. In such situations this maxim is applicable. —सा० 916

673. शीर्षे सर्पो देशान्तरे वैद्य इति न्यायः

Ex. उपरि धनं धनरहितं दूरे दयिता किमेतदापतितम्।
हिमवति दिव्यौषधयः शीर्षे सर्पः समाविष्टः॥

—लौकिकन्याय साहस्री; सा० 682

The serpent is just above the head, while the physician of the snake-bite is far away! If the serpent bites, the poison cannot be removed. This kind of emergency or helpless situation is described in this maxim.

674. शुकनलिकान्यायः

Ex. काकुदीकं शुकनाकमक्षिसन्तर्जनं तथा।
सन्तानं वर्तकं धोरमास्यमोदकमष्टमम्॥

This maxim describes a situation in which some people are frightened unnecessarily without any danger. Some soldiers, sense the danger of attack and take shelter below the chariots on the back of the elephants, though there is no danger of attack. They are 'Śukamohanas'. A female mungoose sitting on the branch of a tree becomes afraid on seeing some birds on the tree. This kind of unnecessary fear is called 'Śukanalikānyāya'.

675. शुण्डासूचिन्यायः

To try to remove a needle, fallen on a street with the help of the trunk of an elephant. This means using heavy means or instruments for a triflling purpose. The maxim indicates this type of human behaviour.

676. शुद्धोदलवणन्यायः

Cf. शकुतिसूत्रन्यायः

This maxim aims at pointing out the difference between individual self and the God which is the same as one between the fresh water and the saline water.

—सा० 819

677. शुष्कतटाकमत्स्यन्यायः

The maxim states that the people do not approach a poor penniless person as the fish do not try to resort to a dried lake.

678. शुष्कस्तनीन्यायः

A simple, ordinary lady observes a beautiful lady having

beautiful form and structure. She has beautiful protruding breasts too. This simple lady feels jealous of her beautiful form says that the well developed breasts actually deforms the body, instead of adoring it. Even the bodice put on them, pricks the breasts. The maxim based on this fact suggests that a person lacking a particular thing jealously condemns the other who possesses it and tries to conceal his want of it by some ridiculous argument.

679. शुष्केष्टिन्यायः

Cf. **भूमिरधिकन्यायः**

The maxim means performing a sacrifice in a dry manner. A disciple may not have correct idea about the procedure or the paraphernalia of a sacrifice. He tries to make prowiso for the articles or uses the articles which are imagined to be those, necessary for it. Neverthess, he slowly acquires the knowledge of the sacrificial procedure.

680. शूकरवाहिकान्यायः

A pig tries to find out a dirty place for movements, even though it enters a beautiful garden which is enriched by lovely, colourful fully-bloomed flowers. The maxim extends this type of behaviour to the wicked persons who target the weak points of the good persons and ignores their good qualities.

—सा० 518

681. शूर्पन्यायः

A winnowing basket throws out unnecessary matter like husk and pieces of stone and retains pure unmixed grain with it. Based on this fact, the maxim describes a good man who discards, or ignores the drawbacks of another man and appreciates his virtues only.

—सा० 321

682. शृङ्गग्राहिकान्यायः

Ex. 1. शृङ्गग्राहिकया श्रुत्या ब्रह्मतापोदिता स्फुटम्.... यथा गोमण्डलस्यां गां शृङ्गं गृहीत्वा विशेषतो दर्शयत्येषा बहुक्षीरेति।

—आनन्दगिरिटीका, बृहदारण्यकोपनिषच्छाङ्करभाष्य, 1.4.866

2. यथा गवादयो विषयाः साक्षाच्छृङ्गग्राहिकया प्रतिपाद्यन्ते प्रतीयन्ते नैवं ब्रह्म।

—भामती, शाङ्करभाष्य, 3.2.22.

(1) In a group of cows, the cowherd can identify a particular man's cow, exactly by catching hold of its horns.

(2) A cow can be controlled by catching its horns. This suggests that one can understand something thoroughly by catching or understanding its important features.

683. शैलूषीन्यायः

Ex. उपमैका शैलूषी सम्प्राप्ता चित्रभूमिकाभेदात्।
प्रीणयति काव्यङ्गे नर्तयति तद्विदां चेतः॥

—चित्रमीमांसा. II.1

Just as an actress assumes different forms, the figure of speech called 'Simile' can assume the form of many other figures of speech (mostlybased on resemblance).

684. श्मशानकुसुमन्यायः

Howsoever fragrant and beautiful they may be, the flowers growing in a burial ground, go in vain, as there is nobody to enjoy or appreciate the beauty and fragrance of those flowers. Similarly, the maxim conveys that a person born in an unhealthy or nasty environment, does not shine, inspite of his merits as there is nobody to appreciate them.

685. श्मशानवैराग्यन्यायः

Ex. प्रमादिनो बहिश्चित्ताः पिशुनाः कलहोत्सुकाः।
संन्यासिनोऽपि दृश्यन्ते देवसन्दूषिताशयाः॥
श्मशानान्ते पुराणान्ते मैथुनान्ते च या मतिः।
सा मतिः सर्वदा काले (चेत्स्यात्) नरो नारायणो भवेत्॥

—हितोपदेश, मित्रलाभ 68; सा० 764

The people who come to the cemetary for cremating the dead body, always enshrine the thought that the human life is momentary and all things are destined to come to an end. They brood over the transitoriness of human life. But the moment they come back, the idea of non-attachment vanish away and all of them get engrossed in the temporary worldly affairs. The maxim insists that a momentary rise of detachment which is a reaction to a certain situation, is never effective.

686. श्यामरक्तन्यायः

The maxim aims at describing the change of situation in human life; observing that whenever the black colour of a jar or a piece of cloth disappears, red colour can be easily applied to them. The situational change is quite natural. —सा० 506

687. श्यालशुनकन्यायः

A person gave the name of his brother-in-law (wife's brother) to his dog, to make his wife angry. He used to abuse the dog uttering his brother-in-law's name. His wife used to become sorrowful, thinking that her husband was abusing her brother only. Really, God is one but a sense of differentiation is deliberately created by giving various names to the same God. Viṣṇu or Śiva are eulogized with some ulterior motive only.

—सा० 136

688. श्येनकपोतन्यायः

Once a pigeon was just coming out of its nest when a falcon attacked it and killed it. The maxim is employed to describe such unexpected, accidental, dangerous situations.

689. श्येनाधिकरणन्यायः

Cf. देवताधिकरणन्यायः, पाष्ठतिर्थगधिकरणन्यायः

Some Vedic injunctions prescribe the deity worship (upāsana). This can be effected even by the superimposed godhood and the injunction of worship can be valid. But this is not correct. Inspite of the worship-oriented injunction, the suggested meaning can be valid, in accordance with the Devatādhikaraṇanyāya. The Śyenādhikarṇanyāya also conveys the same idea.

—सा० 847

690. श्वपुच्छन्यायः

One may try to straighten the tail of a dog but he is never successful. The maxim suggests that the natural shape of a thing can never be changed.

691. श्वशुष्कास्थिन्यायः

A dog goes on chewing a dry bone. It does not stop doing so, even if the blood starts flowing from the injured part in the mouth. Similarly suggests the maxim that a fool always clings on the foolish thing or a useless task. It also throws light on the foolish nature of the stupid persons.

692. श्वसभान्यायः

In a group of dogs, if one starts barking, others also do the same thing. The maxim suggests that men in a group follow their leader, almost instinctively.

693. श्वानमकरन्यायः

Ex. नक्रः स्वस्थानमासाद्य गजेन्द्रमपि कर्षति।
स एव प्रच्युतः स्थानाच्छुनापि परिभूयते॥

—पञ्चतंत्र 3.44.

So long as a crocodile is in the water, it can pull even the elephants into the water. But if it comes out of the water even a dog can assail it. This maxim suggests that if a man is firm in his position, nothing will happen to him. But once he is displaced, even an ordinary fellow will start harassing.

694. श्वानमार्जालन्यायः

The maxim declares that the natural enmity between any two persons remain unabated like the one between a dog and a cat.

695. श्वानशीलन्यायः

Even if the owner beats a dog severly, the dog does not desert him. So also, declares the maxim that it is the nature of a poor, helpless, dependent person.

696. षष्ठाद्यन्यायः

The Mimāṁsā says that in any injunctory passage, the verbal part of the injunction expresses Ārthī Bhāvanā.

It has three aspects—What is be expected—by which and how? The objective expected is the heaven, according to this Ṣaṣṭhādyanyāya which is almost the same as Bhāvārthādhikaraṇa nyāya. —सा० 850

697. षोडशिग्रहणाग्रहणन्यायः

There are two injunctions—one takes the Ṣoḍaśin cup at the time of Atirātra sacrifice; and also one does not take that Ṣoḍaśin cut at the time of Atirātra sacrifice. As the two cannot be reconciled, option (Vikalpa) is permitted here. When one sense is accepted, the other one becomes exception (Paryudāsa).

698. संवादिभ्रमन्यायः

on seeing the lustre of a jewel, somebody develops a delision that it is a jewel only. But actually, he grasps a jewel which catching it. Similarly in "Tattramasi"—तत्त्वमसि-त्वम् is like a lustre of the jewel but while grasping he grasps तत्. तत् is Brahman only. This is an example of concurrent delusion.

699. सक्तुन्यायः

The maxim describes that peevish person who gives up food and subsists on Sattu that is a kind of low type of grain only.

700. सङ्गगुणदोषन्यायः

सन्तताप्तायसि संस्थितस्य पयसो नामापि न ज्ञायते मुक्ता-कारतया तदेव नलिनीपत्रस्थितं राजते।
स्वात्यां सागरशुक्तिकुक्षिपतिते तज्जायते मौक्तिकं प्रायेणोत्तम-मध्यमाधमदशा संसर्गतो जायते।।

—भर्तृहरि, नीतिशतक, 58

The maxim asserts that it is the company which gives rise to virtues or vices in a person. It is rightly said that a man is known by the company he keeps. The rain water drop fallen on hot iron vanishes immediately, it shines like pearls on lotus leaf but it is actually converted into a pearl if fallen in the sea-shell at the time of Svāti nakṣatra.

701. सच्छिद्रघटाम्बुन्यायः

If a jar is porous, all the water poured in it, will flow out from the tiny holes On the basis of this fact the maxim suggests that a man of extra vagant habits looses everything he earns. Even though he earns a lot, his pockets will remain empty because of his spendthrift nature.

702. सन्दशन्यायः

See—मीमांसान्यायप्रकाश with the commentary प्रभा, पृ० 147, 148.

Sandanśa means a forcep. When two organic things are caught, the third one in between them is also caught. This type of grasping is explained by Sandanśa nyāya in Mimānsā.

703. सन्यासियोषान्यायः

According to this maxim, a recluse who has renounced everything in this world and leads a solitary life, cannot have any contact with a woman. It is quite impossible for him to keep any relation with a woman. If he has, then it is a rare wonder!

704. समुद्रमधुबिन्दुन्यायः

The maxim suggests that a little good does not change the nature of the bad, as litte drops of honey does not change the saline test of the sea-water.

705. समुद्रमन्थनन्यायः

When there was churning of ocean the gods and the demons participated. As a result, nectar came out of the ocean-churning which was taken away by the gods. But the ocean was put to extreme hardship. This maxim is used, describing a situation in which one is put to troubles and the other reaps the fruit of it.

706. समुद्रवृष्टिन्यायः

Cf. जलताडनन्यायः, आन्धदर्पणन्यायः, पिष्टपेषणन्यायः

The rain showers do not show any change when they fall in the ocean. Actually the rain should fall on the dry land. The maxim brings out the uselessness of the unnecessary acts.

707. समूहालम्बनन्यायः

This maxim refers to a rule that if it is not possible to relate every word to the sentence severally, one should try to contrue the meaning of all the words. This maxim is more related or rather more connected with the formation of a sentence or to the science of formation of the sentence.

708. सर्वफणन्यायः

A cobra does not remain without raising its hood, even though it is in a very difficult situation. It tries to frighten the people around. Similarly, a man tries to show his resistance even in a very difficult condition. He tries his level best to show his existence even in that troublesome situation.

709. सर्वनाशार्धत्यागन्यायः

Ex. सर्वनाशे समुत्पन्ने ह्यर्धं त्यजति पण्डितः।
अर्धेन कुरुते कार्यं सर्वनाशो हि दुःसहः॥

—पञ्चतंत्र, 4.28

The maxim describes the nature of a wise man who try to save as much as possible when there is a danger of total destruction.

710. सर्वापेक्षन्यायः

The maxim refers to a common practice that all the invitees should come in time to take food. If a person comes late, he will not be served food in that batch. He should wait for the other batch to commence. Joining the lunch in the middle is considered to be out of manners.

711. सलिलभास्करन्यायः-सलिलादित्यन्यायः

यथा सलिलमाविश्य बहुधा भाति भास्करः।
तथा शरीराण्याविश्य बहुधा स्फुरतीश्वरः॥

The sun seems to be multifarious when its reflection is seen in the water. Similarly, one God remains in innumerable bodies, creating an impression that he has innumerable bodies. This is a delusion.

712. सांशयिकनिष्कसांशयिककार्षापणन्यायः

Niṣka is a golden coin which weighs 108 grms Kārṣ āpaṇa is a silver coin of the size of a rupee. But if the availibility of a Niṣka is doubtful and that of a Kārṣ āpaṇa is assured, it should be preferred. The maxim exorts to accept less valuable thing if it is available easily than to wait for the doubtful thing.

'A bird in hand is worth two in the bush'

713. साधुमैत्रीन्यायः

Cf. अपराह्णछायान्यायः

A company of the good man is like the shadow in the day time. It is short in the beginning but gradually it goes on increasing as the time passes on (till the evening).

714. सावकाशनिरकाशन्यायः.

A sentence becomes expectant when there is a possibility of some other matter. The non-expectant injunction undermines the expectant injuction. This can be proved by the two Vedic sentences.

—सा० 64

715. सिंहघण्टान्यायः

This maxim is used to describe a difficult and an impossible task, like that of tying a bell in the neck of a lion.

716. सिंहमृगन्यायः

This maxim is used to describe a permanent, natural enmity between two persons, two religions, two castes, as it exists between a lion and a deer.

717. सिंहमेषन्यायः

Once a shepherd found a small cub of lion. He kept it in the herd of sheep. It began to behave like a sheep only, forgetting its real nature. The maxim based on this incident, suggests that owing to prolonged contact, a man thinks that his body is his soul only.

718. सिंहीक्षीरन्यायः

The milk of a lioness when kept in a golden vessel, shows good effect and proper result. Similarly, the sermons preached by a good preceptor if bestowed on a well controlled, fully enriched disciple will result in good fruit.

—सा० 319

719. सिकताकूपन्यायः

Ex. किंबहुना। सर्वप्रकारेण यथा यथायं वैनाशिकसमय उपपत्तिमत्त्वाय परीक्ष्यते, तथा तथा सिकताकूपवद् विदीर्यत एव। न काञ्चिदत्रोपपत्तिं पश्यामः।

—ब्रह्मसूत्र, शाङ्करभाष्य 2.2.32

The maxim is used to describe some unstable, untenable argument which gives way like the well of sand.

720. सिकतातैलन्यायः

Ex. तैलार्थी हि तिलसर्षपानुपादत्ते न सिकताः।
असत्त्वे च तैलस्य को विशेष सर्षपाणां सिकताभयः॥

—न्यायमञ्जरी, पृ० 473

The maxim speaks about some impossible matters like extracting oil from the sand which is quite improbable and impossible.

721. सुतजन्ममृतिन्यायः

A man got a son by propitiating a deity through his devotion. He wanted another son, so he started propitiating another deity. He got another son but the earlier son was put to death by the anger of the previous deity. The maxim conveys the lesson that even God does not help a greedy person. —सा० 87

722. सुधार्द्रहरिद्रान्यायः

'Sudhā' means white. Haridrā means turmeric which is yellow. But when both of them are mixed, a new red colour is formed. The blendings are wonderful indeed!

723. सुन्दोपसुन्दन्यायः

(1) न चैवं रसभङ्गापत्तिः शान्तशृङ्गारयोश्च विरोधः, इति

रसगङ्गाधरोक्तेः सुन्दोपसुन्दन्यायेनोभयोरपि ध्वंससम्भवा-दिति वाक्यम्।

–अच्युतराव मोडक, साहित्यकार, सरसामोदटीका, पृ० 14

(2) **ननु परस्परविरोधिशीलाः गुणाः सुन्दोपसुन्दवदत् परस्परं ध्वंसना इत्येव युक्त प्रागेव तेषामेक क्रियाकर्तृताम्**

–साङ्ख्यातत्त्वकौमुदी, पृ० 13

The maxim refers to an ancient tale of Sunda and Upasunda, the two demons. They were brothers but started quarrelling with each other for obtaining a nymph called Tilottama. In the strife, both of them died. This hints at the fate of persons, fighting for a worthless cause and ending their lives for nothing.

724. सुपेटिकास्थापनन्यायः

The maxim informs that the devotees keep their (devoted) minds which are like jewels, safely by surrendering them to gods, as valuables are kept in a box for safety.

725. सुप्तडिम्भमुखचुम्बनन्यायः

The maxim brings forth the futility of certain actions, like that of kissing a child when it is asleep. This action is fruitless.

726. सुप्तप्रबुद्धन्यायः

In Bhāgavata I.3, a peculiar point is raised as a prima facie view and then it is refuted. Is there any possility for acquiring the knowledge of the Vedas spontaneously? The final doctrine says that the God only having the knowledge of Self-validity can create the world. But sometimes, however, it is seen that the Vedic knowledge acquired by some one, with the instructions from the preceptors, can repeat it even after getting up from sleep. This change, according to the maxim is likely to form the condition of that of the sleep to awakening.

727. सुभगाभिक्षुकन्यायः

The two words Śubhagā and Bhikṣu cannot be just a posed normally, as they indicate opposite qualities. Once this two approached a third person and asked for refuge in his house. He, out of compassion, gave shelter to Subhagā. The maxim contends that two opposite persons or objects cannot stay together.

—सा० 613

728. सुवर्णन्यायः

हेम्नः संलक्ष्यते ह्यग्नौ विशुद्धिः श्यामिकाऽपि वा॥

—रघुवंश 1.10

The maxim compares gold with a scholar in as much as both of them have to undergo rigorous tests and troubles before establishing their excellence.

729. सूचिकटाहन्यायः

This maxim gives out a common truth that a person does simple acts first and takes up difficult tasks afterwards. Once a person went to a blacksmith and asked him to prepare a frying pan. Another man approached him and asked him to make a needle for him. Obviously, he undertook the easy work of making a needle at the beginning.

—सा० 198

730. सूचिमुखन्यायः

उपदेशो हि मूर्खाणां प्रकोपाय न शान्तये।

—पञ्चतंत्र 1.420; सा० 802

On a winter day, some monkeys were feeling cold.

They wanted to warm up their bodies. All of a sudden, they came across some Gunja fruits. Thinking them to be fire particles, they collected them and began to blow air to brighten them into fire. A sparrow which was observing this fruitless effort, tried to convince the monkeys stating that they were Gunja fruits and not the fire sparks. At this the monkeys were enraged and killed the sparrow in the fury. Citing this example, the maxim conveys that giving advice to the foolish is dangerous and ultimately ends in death.

731. सूत्रबद्धशकुनिन्यायः

Ex. स यथा शकुनिः सूत्रेण प्रबद्धो दिशं दिशं पतित्वा अन्यत्रायतनमलब्ध्वा बन्धनमेवोपाश्रयते, एवमेव खलु सोम्य तन्मनो दिशं दिशं पतित्वा अन्यत्रायतनमलब्ध्वा प्राणमेवाश्रयते प्राणबन्धनं हि सोम्य मन इति।

—छान्दोग्योपनिषद् 6.8.2

When a bird is tied to a string, it tries to make movements; but it can go till the range of the string only. It comes to the same point again and again. Through this example, the maxim suggests that the mind may try to move afar owing to its fickleness, but it comes back ultimately to Praṇa only.

732. सूत्रशाटिकान्यायः

Once a man approached a weaver. He handed over some yarn to him and requested him to weave a cloth for him. "How can he ask for a cloth", thought the weaver. Only after the weaving operation, cloth can be produced and not before that. This is a case of future event which (futuristic action) is mentioned by the maxim.

733. सूर्यास्तन्यायः

When it is said that the sun has set, the idea implied in

it is that the time for the activities of the thieves, paramour and the like has arrived, Similarly when the king of a particular country dies, the time for the enemy to attack that country has come, This idea is indirectly conveyed by the maxim.

734. सैन्धवोदकन्यायः

The matter perceived by the senses dissolves in the senses, as salt put in water gets dissolved in it. On the same lines, all the adjuncts which are false get dissolved; as the serpent notion is dissolved in the rope. The maxim supports the Advaita doctrine.

735. सोपानारोहणन्यायः

The maxim underlines the steady, gradual process of an aspirant who is in search of self. As he steps up he gives up the previous step which is then, identified as the Self. He thus goes on changing and progressing until he reaches the ultimate truth. Thus progress is like stepping up on a staircare. —सा० 44

736. सौधसोपानन्यायः

This maxim is applied to a swift, direct action which is like jumping up to the highest point of a staircase, instead of proceeding step by step.

737. सौभरिन्यायः

A sage called Saubhari married fifty daughters of the king named Māndhāta. He used to have sexual intercourse simultaneously with all these daughters. The maxim speaks of any work of such simultaneous action.

738. स्तनन्धयन्यायः

The maxim contends that a man of detachment who has attained the supreme knowledge, enjoys undisturbed sleep, like a child which sleeps comfortably after sucking its mother's milk.

739. स्तनशल्यपरीक्षान्यायः

The maxim implies the futility of any work which is like placing a small thin bar on the breast of a woman to study the structure of her breast.

740. स्थविरलगुडन्यायः

The old, experienced men may throw a stick, not always at a proper place. The maxim suggests that even an experienced person may commit mistake sometimes.

741. स्थालीपुलाकन्यायः

The maxim is based on a practical observation. Rice is being cooked in a pot. Whether the rice is cooked a grain only is tested. So also, an enlightened person knows not only his real nature but also the entire universe.

—सा० 197

742. स्थानरजङ्गभविसन्यायः

It is believed that if the Vatsanābha poison (very strong poison) is mixed with the poison of other serpent, the effect of that poison is destroyed. The maxim makes use of this practical phenomenaon when the knowledge about the real shell dawns. The superimposed false knowledge of silver is sublated.

743. स्थूणानिखननन्यायः

When a pillar is to be fixed in the ground it is often shaken to see whether it is properly fixed or not. This example gives rise to the maxim and says, when some topics are discussed in a book, a resume of the earlier topics is taken before embarking on the next topics.

744. स्थूलारुन्धतीन्यायः

When the star Arundhatī is to be pointed out some bigger star near it, is shown first because Arundhati star is very small and it is not easily visible. To indicate subtle things, gross things are pointed out first and then attention is drawn to the subtler things—This is what the maxim says.

745. स्नेहदीपन्यायः

If the essential constituent substance perishes the original thing also perishes, as the lamp is extingnished when the oil in the lamp is exhasuted.

746. स्फटिकलौहित्यन्यायः

If a red flower is kept near a crystal, the crystal appearts to be red because of the nearness of the red object. When that flower or the red object is removed, the crystal resumes its original white colour. The individual self appears to be quite different when it is encased in adjuncts. Once the adjuncts are obliterated, its original nature shines.

747. स्रोतोनिम्नन्यायः

The depth of a current cannot be easily grasped. The maxim based on this fact indicates that there are many things which cannot be understood thoroughly.

748. स्वकुचमर्दनन्यायः

(1) निजगुणमहिम्ना सुखाकरः स्यात्
स्वयमनुवर्णयतां सतां न तावत्।
निजकरकमलेन कामिनीनां कुचकलशकलनेन को विनोदः।

(2) आचार्यवान् पुरुषो वेद।

Pressing one's own breasts implies doing one's own flattery. Secondly the ladies feel very happy when their breasts are pressed by their husbands. They do not get any pleasure if they press their own breasts. Similarly, an inquisitive man does not get any knowledge by pondering over something by himself. Only a teacher can give him the pleasure of getting enlightenment, says the maxim. —सा० 346

749. स्वजातिदुरतिक्रमन्यायः

Once a sage was doing ablutions on the bank of Ganga river. Unexpectedly, a female mouse fell down on his lap. The sage took pity on it and converted it into a beautiful lady and looked after it as his own daugher. He tried hard for a suitable bridegroom but that charming damsel didnot like anyone. But when she saw a mouse, she requested the sage to convert her in her previous form again so that she can marry with that mouse. This incident shows that what ever may be his caste he likes it only. Everyone likes his own caste whether high or low..

750. स्वदीपचुम्बनन्यायः

The maxim gives the example of a person who foolishly kisses a burning lamp, thinking that the lamp is his own. When he went near the lamp, he got some burn injuries to his face, lips and to his moustaches. The purport is to decry the practice of being close to somebody, simply because he is his own man.

751. स्वप्नव्याघ्रन्यायः

A tiger seen in a dream state vanishes in the wakeful state. That superimposed tiger is sublated. Similarly, the world seems to be true in the state of ignorance, but it is completely sublated when one acquires the knowledge of the Brahman.

752. स्वप्रकाशाश्रयन्यायः

Though the sun and the sunlight are different, there is a similarity of light or brilliance in them. Therefore, both are supposed to be the same, as they are inseparable. The maxim hints at such inseparable quality.

753. स्वभावसिद्धन्यायः

घृष्टं घृष्टं पुनरपि पुनश्चन्दनं चारुगन्धं
छिन्नं छिन्नं पुनरपि स्वादु चैवेक्षुकाण्डम्।
दग्धं दग्धं पुनरपि पुनः काञ्चनं कान्तवर्णं
न प्राणान्ते प्रकृतिविकृतिर्जायते ह्युत्तमानाम्॥

The sandalwood does not give up its fragrance, even though it is rubbed, broken, cut or pasted. The gold does not give up its lustre or shining even though it is burnt in the burning fire. Similarly, the good people do not give up their nature though put to excruciating trouble. On the strength of these examples the maxim speaks about the good behaviour of greatmen.

754. स्वेदजनिमित्तशाटिकत्यागन्यायः

The insects take their rise in sweat. The clothes are affected by these worms and they are seen occupying all the clothes. Then how thoughtless the act of throwing away all the clothes will be! The maxim is applied to such thoughtless action.

755. हंसकाकन्यायः

इभतुरग-शतैः प्रयान्ति मूढा
गुणवन्तो विबुधाश्चलन्ति पद्भ्याम्।
गिरिशिखरगतापि काकपङ्क्तिः
पुलिनगतैर्न समेति राजहंसैः॥

A swan may be sitting on the sands down below, while

a group of crows may be sitting high up on the top of the mountain. Can there be any comparison between a crow and a swan? Similarly, the maxim suggests that there are many wicked persons in the world and the good are very few. But the number here is not at all important.

756. हंसक्षीरन्यायः

The maxim indicates the nature of the good men who accept and appreciate good qualities of men and ignore or give up their faults, by giving the example of a swan which separates water from the milk from their mixture and drinks only the milk leaving the water content behind.

757. हंसबकन्यायः

If a swan enters a flock of cranes, its real worth is not recognised as both are white in colour. When the cranes come to know that he has come all the way from Mānasa lake, they ask him to describe it. The Mānas lake is full of crystal clear wateı, golden and precious jewels was the description given by the swan but when the cranes came to know that there are no frogs in the lake, they laugh at the swan and form a very adverse opinion about the lake. The maxim suggests that similarity of colour cannot be a criterian of greatness. The cranes have no idea about the precious jewels—their lustre, value and greatness—so they do not think anything better than the frogs. —सा० 75

758. हस्तामलकन्यायः

ब्राह्मणः साक्षादुपलब्ध्यर्थ मुपासनार्थं च हृदयाकाशः स्थानमुच्यते शालग्राम इव विष्योः। तस्मिन् हि तद् ब्रह्मोणास्यमानं मनोमय त्वादिधर्मविशिष्टं साक्षादुपलभ्यते पाणाविवामलकम्।

—शांकरभाष्य, तैत्तिरीयोपनिषद् 6, उपोद्घात

A maxim of putting a myrobolan fruit (Āmalakī fruit) on the palm. The truth, being round in shape, canbe seen thoroughly from all sides. The perfect, complete knowledge of any man about any object, is compared to the complete knowledge of a myrobolan fruit on the palm of hand. –सा० 280

759. हिरण्यनिधिन्यायः

The maxim suggests that the men who often go to the Brahmaloka have no idea about the Brahmaloka. There is a good deal of wealth in the womb of the earth. But the people walking on the surface of the earth have no idea about it.

760. हेरम्बनरसिंहन्यायः

The maxim intends to paint a picture of a situation when mutually opposite things come together. The idol of Gaṇeśa is a combination of an elephant and a man. The elephant and the lion partially occupy the bodies of Gaṇeśa and Narasimha partially. The theory of Anekānta of the Jainas is a set of many opposite concepts like is and is not. –सा० 707

761. ह्रदनक्रन्यायः

Forest and tiger; lake and crocodile promote the existence of other. If they are separated, they will be the victims of the foresters (hunters and fishermen) Their togetherness provide a strong protection to them. The maxim emphasizes that the natural co-existence is always beneficial. –सा० 392

Appendix

Here is a list of Nyāyas, the detailed information is not available to me.

1. अनुकूलाचलन्याय:
2. अन्धगोक्षेत्रन्याय:
3. आख्वंक्षपिटकन्याय:
4. कज्जलन्याय:
5. कुक्षिस्थमक्षिकान्याय:
6. कूष्माण्डस्तेयन्याय:
7. कृत्वाचिन्तान्याय:
8. गृहार्थमारोपितस्य दीपस्येतिन्याय:
9. चित्रानलन्याय:-चित्राङ्गनान्याय:
10. चित्रामृतनयाय:-चित्राङ्गनान्याय:
11. पटाच्छादनन्याय:
12. पृष्ठखलीनन्याय:
13. यूपरशनान्याय:
14. वालकर्कटन्याय:
15. षाष्ठतिर्यगधिकरणन्याय:
16. समाक्षिप्तकाष्ठन्याय:
17. सूकरवाटिकान्याय:-शूकरवाटिकान्याय:

Alphabetical Index (वर्णानुक्रमणिका)

✦✦✦